Nightmare Memoir

Claude J. Letulle

Nightmare Memoir

Four Years as a Prisoner of the Nazis

Foreword by Amos Perlmutter

Impact Christian Books, Inc.
Kirkwood, Missouri

Copyright @ 1998 by Claude Leutlle
All rights reserved

No portion of this book may be reproduced in any form or by any means without the express written consent of the author or the publisher. Brief passages may be quoted without permission in the body of reviews for the limited purpose of reviewing this book. For more information, contact the publisher.

Originally published in hardcover by Louisiana State University Pres!

Library of Congress Number 87-3878

ISBN 0-89228-191-X

Printed in the United States

Impact Christian Books, Inc.
332 Leffingwell Avenue
Kirkwood, MO 63122
314-822-3309
www.impactchristianbooks.com

Contents

Foreword	vii
Publisher's Note	ix
Prologue	xii
Nightmare Memoir	13
Epilogue	192
Official Documents	193
The Author's Medals	196
Map	198

Foreword

Amos Perlmutter

Nightmare Memoir, by Claude Letulle, is a harrowing, human document, a personal testimony of and witness to man's almost casual-and certainly callous-inhumanity to man. This personal document, told without embellishment in simple, almost brutally direct language, is Kafkaesque in its recitation of the horrors visited on the victims of the Nazi terror.

Letulle was a French soldier taken prisoner by the Nazis in the wake of the crushing French defeat in World War II. His account of serving, or rather being forced to serve, in a camp where the Nazis performed gruesome medical experiments on their prisoners is painful to read. Its very straightforwardness, its lack of interpretation and literary style, serves to make it that much more powerful. Letulle's book was not written for intellectual, literary, or political purposes. It seems more like a personal act of exorcism on the part of Letulle, and indeed, that is exactly what it is.

Letulle's staccato and primitive writing brings a sense of awful urgency to his stories and descriptions of events. He appears to have no interest in the ideological, philosophical, or political backgrounds or justifications for these experiments. Neither does he take the novelist's approach of creating horror fiction. He simply states; the facts and the reality that constitute his telling are more devastating than any invented tales or philosophical musings.

As prisoner, Letulle was assistant, helper, and nurse at an "experimental" hospital in which victims were tortured and used as human guinea pigs for medical experiments conducted to further the cause of "racial science." He writes of perverted Nazi doctors, brutal female nurses, and their pathetic subjects, and he describes the maniacal sexual experimentation that caused disfigurement and death. The experiments almost defied any definition of horror, and Letulle was witness to them all. I wonder whether any reader can get through his narrative without emitting a cry of pain.

This book is one of the most painful I have ever had to read, precisely because it is so unadorned, so bereft of the protectiveness of literary style or historical or political interpretation. It just is, a book that rumbles with awful life and the truth of experience. It does not seek to redress, to remind others, to punish, or to warn against the evils of nazism. However, in sharing his experience with readers, Letulle has shared the pain of it intimately enough to perhaps induce nightmares in the readers—nightmares not easily shed. In the process of reading his narrative, we all share in the burden. We may feel relief in not having had to experience Letulle's nightmares literally, but we are never quite the same after experiencing them on the printed page.

In a way, Claude Letulle is Everyman. He was not a Jew, not a Gypsy, not a Bolshevik or Slav, not a member of any group singled out for torture, death, and extermination by the Nazis. Yet, because of the war, he was a living and livid witness to Nazi crimes. The book is a testament to Letulle's will to survive and, intended or not, a needed reminder of the horror that was nazism.

Original Publisher's Note

The decision to publish *Nightmare Memoir* was not an easy one. I have not decided whether the task was difficult because the story was hard to believe, or because it was all too easy to believe.

I was part of the generation that came along immediately after World War II. For us, growing up in the comfort and security of the United States, the atrocities recounted in this book are totally alien. "These things could not have happened; human beings are not capable of this," you tend to say to yourself. "If this really happened, it was an aberration; acts of barbarism by a few, now long dead."

The story, unfortunately, is true. The facts, names and places have been corroborated by military historians who have reviewed the manuscript. Claude Letulle's imprisonment has also been documented by the French government. At the end of his four-year long ordeal, the French government awarded Mr. Letulle the Croix de Guerre and the Medaille Militaire.

A half century has gone by since the events of this book. Claude Letulle is now a retired chemist who lives quietly with his wife in Jackson, Louisiana. In my many discussions with him about his experiences and recent events in Europe, we always return to a debate about the human condition and the future of the human race. "Surely these things could never happen again," I usually say. He looks down and shakes his head sadly, "You do not understand, you just do not understand." He then looks up with an intensity that is startling. "These things *will* happen again." The depth of feeling is palpable and utterly convincing in its passion.

—*Stephen E. Covell, Charleston Press*

Prologue

Claude Letulle was a student when France declared war on Germany in September, 1939. The son of a doctor, he was expected to follow in his father's footsteps. Instead, he had his own plans to study law and set up an office in Nice, on the Mediterranean Sea.

Shortly after the declaration of war, Letulle returned with his family from a vacation at the Riviera and immediately received his military induction orders. As he left for duty, he vowed to his fiancee that the war would be short and he would soon come back to her.

After basic training, Letulle was sent to a tank unit in the Seine-Marne area. Three months later he was transferred to the front. On May 9, his unit marched to Sedan, on the German border, and on the following day, the German attack broke down the entire defense. Several days later, in the turmoil of retreat, Letulle was captured. At the time of his capture he was twenty years old.

The author in 1939, a few months before his induction into the French Army

To the memory of all the American soldiers who gave their lives in France to achieve freedom

Nightmare Memoir

When this story begins, World War II had been going on for less than a year, and France was convinced of her strength. She hoped to repress the Germans easily, unsuspecting of the enormity of Hitler's plan. I was a corporal in the 10th Regiment of Cuirassiers, 3rd Heavy Armor Division. At the beginning of May, 1940, we were in the region of Ardennes, 180 miles southeast of Dunkirk, on the way to Sedan. On May 9, our lieutenant informed us that a few Germans armed with machine guns had penetrated the French territory but that they would soon be overcome. More than fifty years later, I can still hear his confident voice.

That morning we had been expecting to have breakfast when we discovered that the kitchen mobile unit had disappeared. As we were bemoaning our hunger and speculating on the whereabouts of the mobile unit, rumors began to circulate that the Germans were advancing, attacking with gas. We became alarmed, for we had no masks. The officer of our division quickly ordered the masks, which reached us in less than an hour. Overlooking the fact that masks come in different sizes, the sergeant went swiftly about distributing them. I received one too small and with the elastic band missing. It was useless. Fortunately, the gas attack did not occur.

During the afternoon we reached Sedan. We were received like conquerors, though we hadn't seen one German. The population, deliriously happy to see us, made everything available to us free of charge. I visited a local bar where, naturally, we all drank too much. In the course of a vigorous argument I–still wearing my helmet–received a blow that bounced me against the wall and shattered the helmet. Had I been on the battlefield, the cheap metal helmet could not have protected me against a shell. I felt a small wave of fear–first our breakfast, then the mask, now the helmet. What was going on?

On the following morning the Germans attacked at daybreak with everything they had. We were immediately forced to the ground by a barrage of bombs. The bombers, Heinkel III and Junker 88, were firing all around while the Stukas flew low, blowing their sirens at us. The loud sound was new to us, and we were becoming panicky. When the bombing stopped, the tanks began to advance over every inch of ground with the intention of finishing off as many of us as possible. We had no means to resist, and the situation was desperate. Our French army had been routed, and the place was wide open for the enemy to penetrate. With the enemy right behind us, our appalling retreat began. The idea of falling into German hands was terrifying; chaos and anguish ruled as every man fled.

Over the next several days, a few companions and I, separated from our original unit, joined up with other units and fought the Germans as best we could. Always we were beaten back and had to resume our retreat. On May 19 we fought in the town of Chambry, and on the next day we reached the little town of Parfondru just ahead of a regiment of French infantry, whom we promptly joined. The commandant heard an SOS on the radio: Five miles away, an infantry unit of about 250 men was almost completely surrounded by Germans and needed emergency ammunition. The commandant mobilized four tanks loaded with ammunition and asked for volunteers. I was the only one.

We left on our mission under heavy fire, and when we were only one and a half miles from the endangered infantry unit, shells began to fall all around us. Our hindmost tank was hit, and because of its extra load of ammunition, the explosion was immense. As we approached the unit, I saw some of the men hiding behind the ruins of the village. I got down from the tank I was riding and hid behind a nearby wall. There I met the captain, who told me to unload the ammunition quickly. Our tanks took their positions, and soon the unit was well armed. After a period of intense fighting, the Germans temporarily ceased firing in order to regroup. The infantry unit took that opportunity to escape and join our regiment at Parfondru.

Back in Parfondru, we were soon completely surrounded by Germans, and though we had little chance against them, we organized a resistance. In the course of our opposition, a sergeant was wounded at my side. Under heavy fire I carried him to a house close by and left him with some Red Cross attendants. As I was opening the door to leave, I saw several Germans standing only a few yards away. They had already caught many of our men. I quickly closed the door and walked out through the back door, which led to the stable. I reached the barn undetected, and as I was deciding whether to take refuge in the hayloft, a ladder was lowered before me. Someone ordered me to climb fast because the Germans were very close. Reaching the attic, I saw at least ten other French soldiers. For the moment we were safe.

The intermittent firing had ceased, and we could hear only some vehicular noise as the German convoys passed. In our hideout we made an opening to the roof so that we could see outside. Nothing happened during the night, and no one slept.

The following morning, we saw the German infantry in all the strategic places as the town became occupied. I saw a local civilian in front of his house shake hands with a German officer. His action so angered me that I instantly took aim at him with my rifle. My companions wisely, and quickly, stopped me before I could shoot, for the gunfire would have given us away.

Right next to the barn roof was a telephone post. As the Germans moved from town to town, they quickly set communication lines; thus, having that post so near to our refuge concerned us. Even as we were discussing it, a German soldier climbed the post and set a line. Going back down the post, he peered suspiciously at the attic. Just as he was preparing to toss a grenade at our barn, an officer called him. We had escaped; but our refuge was not safe, and we decided that we must leave during the night.

The days were beginning to be hot. Although we had not had food for a day or two, we suffered more from thirst. About midnight, when everything was calm, we considered crossing the short distance behind the barn to some woods. But between the barn and the woods lay a field in which the Germans had made camp. It was too risky. The better alternative seemed to be the main street on the front side of the barn, even though there would be Germans in every house. All ten of us armed ourselves and left. Reaching the street, we saw that the windows in the houses were wide open and the Germans inside were singing. We inched forward, crawling along the walls, and eventually reached the woods. We then chose a direction that seemed to be north, hoping to locate our unit in Laon.

For four days we walked by night through the marshland, exposed to a full moon, eaten up by mosquitoes, suffocating in the heat, and without any real nourishment, until exhaustion overcame us. During the fifth day I heard a truck passing close by and determined that if there were a road, I would find a farm on it and possibly some food or water. I had walked only a few steps when I heard dogs barking and saw a German patrol coming my way. I threw myself into the marsh, sunk in up to my ears, and madly attempted to drink some of the stagnant water. The patrol passed without the dogs smelling me. Once they were out of sight, I took a long breath and continued my walk. I finally found the road and saw a farm a little farther on. Since daylight was a poor time to move, I decided to wait until night to approach it.

The next morning I hid behind the well at the farm and was at the point of walking to the house when I saw two German soldiers leaving it. They bypassed the well without noticing me and left. I crawled to the chicken coop, and as I opened the door, a man spoke from somewhere nearby.

"You there, what are you doing in there? Get out of here fast. Go! I have some Germans in my house, and if they find you here they will kill me."

"But sir, I'm dying of thirst. Can't you give me a little water and some food that I can take with me to the woods?"

He refused to listen and threatened to call the Germans. I don't know what kept me from killing him with my bayonet. I think that he understood my feelings and he ran away, yelling. Swiftly, I returned to hide behind the well. Three Germans had heard the screams and rushed from the house. They saw me and opened fire but did not hit me. I threw a grenade that silenced them and the farmer, and I ran as fast as I could. Within minutes other Germans were chasing me. I did not want to lead them to the woods where my companions were hidden, so I went in another direction, running faster than I had ever done in my life. Finally, out of breath and incapable of another step, I stopped. I had lost them, but I had also lost my companions and I was alone. My stomach was hurting and the thirst was unbearable. I picked some leaves from a tree and sucked on them before falling asleep. During the night, a chill woke me and I lay awake. In the morning, I began to walk but I was hopelessly lost. For two more days I wandered as despair gradually took hold of me.

On the third morning, some noises woke me up. I tensed and lay still. I couldn't believe my eyes as four of my companions stood in front of me. We had been traveling in the same direction. The group had divided to facilitate the escape and reduce the danger of being caught. Being with them again revived my courage, though they were no better off than I. Half-starved, dying of thirst, with ragged, filthy uniforms, they spoke of surrender but did nothing about it.

We resumed our dreary routine, waking by night and hiding by day. One evening we stopped near a town. I crawled close to a signpost and read the word *Chambry*, and remembered that we had been there earlier during the retreat. Therefore, we were heading east and had walked some thirty miles in the wrong direction. We were incredulous, but that night we started in another direction, thinking that this time we were going south. For many days we continued, hardly able to move apace while we burned with fever.

On the morning of June 22, we woke to the sound of German voices and discovered that we had spent the night near a German camp. We began to crawl, hoping to escape, when a guttural voice ordered us to stop. Several Germans surrounded us and pointed their machine guns in our faces, appearing ready to shoot. One of them came to me and offered me a cigarette, but I refused (I had heard that the Germans gave poisoned cigarettes to prisoners). They ordered us to walk to their camp, near a building I recognized as the city hall. They had converted the city hall into their general quarters, and the Nazi flag was floating at the door.

I was taken to the general quarters and pushed into a room, where I found myself facing several officers. They stood up to greet me and motioned me to sit down and wait. I understood that they wanted to feed me, and I was happy just to be permitted to sit on a chair. In a few minutes a soldier brought a plate and left it on the floor before me. I began to swallow food as fast as I could, but one of the officers, who spoke awkward French, told me to eat slowly or else I could become very sick. I was muddy up to my ears, with a stinking, three weeks beard, and my clothes were so torn that one could only guess that they had once been a uniform.

After eating, I was allowed to shave and bathe under surveillance and was then taken under guard to a barn to rest. I must have slept a full day, but I don't know for certain. A soldier finally wakened me and motioned for me to follow him outside, where many other prisoners, including my four companions, were gathered. Soldiers in green uniforms surrounded us and ordered us to start walking.

The walk had to be made in absolute silence, and any prisoner caught saying even a single word would be shot dead. Our guards all appeared to be in their forties, veterans of World War I. They felt nothing but hatred for the French.

As soon as we left town, they began to show their cruelty, constantly insulting and cursing us, and stopping their bicycles to beat us at random with their gun butts. They forced us to walk at a good speed, and after three hours the pace proved to be more than our exhausted bodies could stand. We motioned that we needed to rest, and they replied by increasing their blows. In a silent, mutual agreement, we all stopped walking at the same time. Confronted with such resistance, one of the guards came directly to me and hit me so hard with his gun that I fell unconscious, whereupon he continued to jab me mercilessly with his bayonet. I slowly regained consciousness.

"Get up immediately and keep walking or I'll kill you," he said, shouting in a voice trembling with fury. My companions tried to help me get up, but other guards prevented them. Dizzy, half-conscious, and racked with pain, I got to my feet with great difficulty. The march recommenced. To ensure that we would walk, the soldiers kept striking us.

One seemed to take special pleasure in beating me.

As we walked, our strength drained away. My feet had begun to feel very sore, my neck was stiff and swollen, and my face was cut up from the blows. I burned and ached and, worst of all, I was again very thirsty—insanely thirsty.

The guards took many breaks and made a great display of enjoying their food and water, all the while laughing at us. Late in the afternoon, one of them came to us and declared that he would be more than happy to give us a little water. We chose to believe him because we were going out of our minds for want of water. He stopped us and with an ugly smile handed his canteen to the first man in line. When the prisoner reached for it, the German pulled it back and emptied the full canteen on the ground. It would have been enough to satisfy our thirst for a little while, and his deceitfulness made us feel worse. He knew it and looked us over with amusement. I wished then to choke him to death. I knew that would have meant my instantaneous death, and so I decided that I would kill him if ever I had the opportunity. Silently, we resumed the walk.

Night came and the guards ordered us to rest. We had reached Laon, a town that had a population of about twenty thousand. But with the Germans near, everyone had fled. The soldiers forced us into the church, where my first thought was to look for holy water. There was none, but there were hundreds of other French prisoners. A few of them had somehow gotten a little water that, understandably, they held onto jealously and refused to share with anyone. All the men were starved, like us. One of them told me that twice a week the Germans would throw a few loaves of bread inside-that was all. Only the prisoners near the door, and those able to rush forward quickly enough, could hope to get some; therefore, hundreds of prisoners had not had anything to eat in more than a week.

I was doomed to spend a week confined in that church, but fortunately, I didn't know it then. I looked for an empty pew and lay down. I felt happy just to be able to stretch and rest. Soon, however, my neck began to hurt so badly that I could hardly move my head, and I began to fear that I had some broken bones. Later I decided to take off my shoes. My feet were swollen and bleeding, and my shoes were worn out, though I was certain that we would have much more walking to do.

The following day the main door of the church was opened wide. A few Germans, well armed, kept us in order while a few others threw some twenty loaves of bread into the portal. For the few prisoners who were standing close by, the bread signaled a fight for survival. For some two hundred others there was only another three days of starvation. I was one of them. But three days later, when again a few loaves were thrown, I managed to get my little share. The Germans enjoyed the sight of the French soldiers fighting for a piece of bread, and they laughed at the despair on our faces. Worse than that, we had not been given a single drop of water, and the thirst was intolerable. Were they trying to let us die of thirst? I felt as if my body had become a hardened, dried-up sponge.

One morning soon after, we were suddenly taken outside. Greeting us were four machine guns. Several prisoners panicked and ran. When the guards called at them to stop, the poor men only ran faster and were shot.

We were ordered to start walking, again in silence. Where were we going? What was to be the outcome of this war? We were now at the end of June, and I had been without news for many days, though I realized that my country was probably occupied at least in part by the Nazis. We walked. The weak prisoners fell helplessly and were beaten with gun butts and jabbed ferociously. If they did not respond, they were immediately shot. We spent the first night along the road, and I was haunted by the idea of escape. An attempt would be futile, of course, since the guards' vigilance was extreme.

During the next few days my strength and courage failed me. We covered an average of twenty miles a day, exhausted and deprived of food and water. The bodies of those shot for dragging behind or falling down from sickness were left behind. But our numbers did not diminish, for in every town we passed, new prisoners were added to our group.

One evening it began to rain, the first time since my capture. It rained hard enough to soak our uniforms and to fill the ditches, from which we gulped that night when we stopped. I tried to rest, but that was not so easy because my face and neck were covered with blisters and pus from the blows I had received. My shoes were nearly disintegrated, and my feet were bleeding. After a week and a half of walking and torment, I had had it.

In the morning I could not get up, and some companions helped me to my feet. I walked no more than a hundred yards when I fell down and thought that I was going to die. But one does not die so easily.

Before my friends could help me up, a soldier came over and hit me so violently in the back that I screamed.

My reaction apparently gave him such pleasure that he crushed my left hand under his boot. Several prisoners immediately encircled the guard with such a menacing attitude that he walked away. Most of the skin on my left hand was torn away, and though my friends had helped me up, the blows to my back made it difficult for me to remain upright. However, my fear of death by torture outweighed my pain, and so I walked on.

After nearly two weeks we reached Luxembourg, and I knew then that we were headed for a German prisoner camp. I thought of the misery many of us had endured already, and I wondered what was ahead. The capital city appeared to be deserted; all windows and doors were closed. Eventually some old women came along, carrying baskets of food. They approached us and began to offer the food, but the guards quickly attacked them and beat them. The guards then stepped on the food until nothing left was edible. Watching them, I was reminded of the Romans who had thought themselves masters of the world.

After Luxembourg, the guards doubled their vigilance, and the idea of escaping left me completely, for it would have been impossible to move one foot away without being shot. It rained once in a while, refreshing us and providing us with drinking water. Otherwise we had none. One night after stopping, I found some water in a ditch and foolishly drank it from empty preserve cans. Predictably I began to feel stomach pains soon afterwards.

On the next morning, when I woke up, I thought I would never move again as my whole body pulsated violently with pain. My neck was still swollen and my left hand, like my face, was full of pus. My back pain had increased, and my feet, with the soles of my shoes completely gone, showed signs of infection. The only thing I could do for myself was to tear one leg off my pants for foot bandages.

A few miles beyond the city, the Germans ordered a number of us to stop on a small plateau surrounded by low hills where machine guns were installed. I could not figure out what the Germans had in mind, but I knew, because of the filth, that other prisoners had been there. We had only just stopped when I saw lying on the ground nearby a small piece of sheet iron, which I quickly grabbed and began fashioning into a cup. It was raining hard, and with my new cup I managed to drink all I wanted. I examined my wounds, and when I took off my shoes, the skin was stuck to the leather. I had made a mistake, but my feet were hurting too much, and what good was it for me to walk with soleless shoes? I realized that I would not be able to put my shoes back on, and so I tore a piece of my coat lining and bandaged my feet with it.

It rained steadily, and I looked around for anything that might make a shelter for the night. I found a few pieces of wood and piled some grass on top, enough to cover my face and part of my chest. It rained all night, and the following morning I woke up soaked. We still had nothing to eat, but since I had drunk quite a bit of water, I felt a little better.

Running through my mind continually were the possible tortures I might have to suffer once we reached Germany. I was absorbed in thought when a few guards came along and, faithful to their bestial habits, began to beat us. "Get up. Fast, fast!" they demanded. We had walked a few minutes when I felt a hand holding me by the collar. I turned around to face a guard, pointing his rifle at me. He told me to remove the bandages around my feet, and since disobeying him would mean death, I sat down on the wet ground and began to unravel the wrappings. I had hardly finished when another guard walked up with a piece of barbed wire in his hand. Before I imagined what he might have in mind, he beat my feet with the wire. The blood gushed, and he stopped as the other soldier, still pointing his gun at me, ordered me to get up and start walking. The pain was excruciating, but I got up, even though I feared that I might faint. One of the guards stayed close to me, making certain that I would not rest or sit down. My feet felt like two large, shapeless blocks. When they stopped bleeding, I began to feel a renewed pulsation of pain through my body.

After walking awhile I saw at a distance some officers handing out food that, incredibly, looked like meat. As I went closer, I realized that it was meat-rotten meat full of live worms and giving off a putrefying odor. The prisoner ahead of me suddenly went mad. As he was handed the meat, he caught the German officer and rubbed the meat into his mouth. The officer freed himself and shot blindly. The prisoner fell, but he was not dead until two guards came over and finished him. Many of us tried to assault the guards, but the shots over our heads quieted us. I accepted my portion of meat and threw it away as soon as I could. After limping a little farther, I paused quickly to bandage my feet with tattered shreds of cloth from my filthy jacket.

The following morning the rain stopped and the day turned hot. I was feverish and thirsty and my legs felt like trunks of lead. During the day we had an unexpected rest break, and I was very happy to be able to sit down in a nearby ditch and repair my foot bandages.

Only seconds after I reached the ditch, several hundred prisoners began shouting wildly and running across the road. What could be the matter? Then I saw that some of them had killed two cows in the field and were drinking the blood. I hadn't the stomach to go for my share, but I understood how they felt. The German guards saw everything but didn't move or even speak. With hatred on their faces, they let the prisoners do as they pleased. As for me, the condition of my feet was so bad that I was afraid of tetanus, and I knew very well that I could not hope to receive any attention if that developed. A few minutes later, we were ordered to start moving again.

On the following day I figured that we were close to the German border because the guards seemed .nervous and kept shouting at us to walk faster until we were nearly running in the rain. Finally at nightfall, when we stopped, I was so exhausted that I fell into a ditch full of water and didn't move all night.

The next morning we awoke to the sound of machine guns, and the guards ordered us to move at the same speed as the day before. I had not even bothered to bandage my feet because in my desperation I no longer cared. During the day we were given enough bread for each prisoner to have some. I ate my ration, but I had dysentery and was beginning to feel renewed stomach pains.

Another day passed and finally we reached Treves on the German border, a strategic city with a population of about fifty-eight thousand. The Germans wanted to display their victory by the number of prisoners they were bringing in, and so they marched us to the downtown area, where a special reception had been prepared for us. Every window in sight was covered with a Nazi flag, and the crowd was so dense and nearly uncontrollable that it seemed that every person in the city was there to see us. A mob of children in Nazi uniforms had baskets of stones that they threw at us, and the women who were close enough spat in our faces and drenched us with buckets full of dirty water, urine, and excrement. Only the men of the city were impassive. They looked at us with hard faces, but without hostility. Our guards, encouraged by the popular demonstration, increased their strokes to make us run faster. Several prisoners were so sick and exhausted that they fell dead. As we walked over their bodies, the crowd's exuberance seemed limitless. For some reason, I was spared the blows; otherwise, I, too, would probably have joined the dead.

Treves is situated along the Rhine valley. We headed for a camp on one of the few hills near the city. The road to the top was steep, and only the guards' blows made us climb, one foot at a time. Although I received few blows, I barely managed to climb, or even to remain conscious. When we arrived, the gates to the camp were wide open and we walked right in. The camp was a simple arrangement of barracks, each containing several bunks. After so many days of insane struggle, I threw myself into a bunk, savoring the luxury of a plain straw mattress.

As I relaxed I began to wonder at the Nazis' display of great military strength. Maybe they had subdued all of Europe. It had been at least a month since I had been separated from my unit and from all news of the outside world. How long would my captivity last? A few months? Some years? For life? Was there not in this world a country powerful enough to beat the Nazis back? My mind grew fuzzy, and I drifted into a sleep that lasted for more than forty hours. I was awakened by the usual beating with a gun butt. The guard shouted, "Up, right away, you. Go and eat."

I was feeling better for having rested, but when I tried to stand, my feet were too sore and infected, and my ankles were swollen. I tried again and managed to get up. Outside I saw a mobile kitchen unit where food distribution was in progress. One soldier handed me a mess kit, the next one filled my plate with a weak soup, and the next gave me two slices of German bread and a tiny piece of margarine; but there was nothing to drink. I carefully held my meal and returned to my bed to enjoy it properly. After having been nearly starved for so many days, I felt it was a feast. After eating, I went back to sleep, feeling satisfied. Soon after, I woke up with strong abdominal pains and was very grateful that in this camp there were latrines.

On the following day the bread was eliminated from our ration. I was so weak that I decided to stay in bed and rest except when the soup was served, once a day. The wretched soup was so much better than nothing that I looked forward to it. The rest was good for me, and I thought that if I could spend a couple of weeks in the camp, I might recuperate from most of my ailments. My feet were not hurting me half so much, and my left hand looked much better; but my neck was still swollen, and I could not move my head. The camp seemed like a paradise, since I had really not thought that my luck would take me so far. Those four days following my long sleep did me much good.

Early on the fifth day, we were awakened in the customary manner and told to be up and out. The guards lined us up for attention and began a count. It lasted for several hours as they counted us more than twenty times. After noon an officer quietly appeared and examined every one of us from head to foot without ever uttering a word. Finally, he silently turned and left, just as he had come. A few minutes later the guards began beating us with gun butts, our signal to start moving. We went through the gate toward the city. Soon they began jabbing us to make us go faster, so that we ended up running all the way down the hill. By the time we reached the city, the old wounds on my feet had reopened.

The population quickly gathered along the way, happy to have another chance to insult us. Since they'd had no advance notice, they hadn't been able to prepare for us. So we were spared another reception of stones and excrement, but still they spat on us.

When we reached the railroad station, a French cattle train awaited us, our first sign that France had fallen to the Nazis. All my hopes were stifled. The cattle wagon had solid walls, a door on each side, and grills at both ends. It could hold about forty men, but at the point of a gun we were forced to pack together until seventy-five of us were inside. The door was locked from the outside. It was a hot June day, and we were jammed so tightly against one another that it was barely possible to catch a breath and impossible to move. A new phase of our torture had begun.

We spent the rest of the day suffocating in the wagon. With nightfall, some cool air penetrated the grills. Sleep was impossible as the night crawled on. Nature caught up with us during the night, and the dysentery from which many, like myself, were suffering produced an odor that filled the wagon, causing men to faint against each other. We endured without food, water, or even an opening of the door to give us fresh air.

By the morning of the second day, the train had not yet moved. The heat and smell were unbearable. We were deliriously thirsty and at least two men were dead. I was weak and nauseated from the odor of my rags, and though my legs could no longer hold me, I was in no danger of falling down. During the afternoon the wagon jerked and I hoped that we would soon be moving, but nothing else happened. At dark we began to move, and the train rolled all night without stopping.

The next morning when the train stopped, the guards who had been sitting on top of the wagons opened the doors but warned us to stay put. The odor was so bad that it succeeded in nauseating them. Furious and cursing, they hurried away, calling us pigs. We were grateful for the open wagon door, which at least helped the odor to evaporate.

After a while, a guard came to the open door and pushed against the few prisoners nearest it, enough to make room for a bucket of drinking water. Since we were unable to move, the badly needed water could not be passed around, and only those near the door had a chance to drink. I was too far inside the wagon. Shortly the guard returned for the bucket, but when he saw that it was still full, he went into a rage and told us that since we were not thirsty, there would be no more drinking water. He picked up the bucket and slammed the door. The train began to move again after dark. During the night I lightly dozed until a jerky stop woke me up. I heard many prisoners gasping for breath. The man in front of me was dead.

The following morning, the fourth day, the train stopped at a railroad station and the wagon doors were opened. Before the guards realized what was happening, the prisoners who had any strength remaining rushed out, stepping over the sick and the dead in their eagerness to get fresh air. In less than a minute, all of them were on the platform and the ground nearby. The surprised guards did not even reach for their guns. They could see that we were determined to remain outside, and they seemed to be afraid of us.

While I sat on the grass, I saw two of the guards go into our wagon to pick up the dead, holding them by their feet as they dragged them to a ditch near the track. A bread truck pulled up, backing off the road and stopping close by. Three soldiers got out and tossed bread onto the platform for us. After unloading, they returned to the truck, and it left as abruptly as it had come. There was enough bread for all the prisoners to have as much as they wanted, and for a while we rested as we pleased. But our freedom puzzled me, and I expected something ominous to happen.

I had eaten until I was satisfied, and I was enjoying lying on the ground when our French cattle train, now completely empty, moved away without the guards paying any attention to it. Shortly after that, an uncovered coal train backed up in our direction and stopped on the track beside us. The guards assumed their usual dispositions and, with the viciousness of wild animals catching prey, stampeded us into the wagons.

The new wagon was about the size of the previous one, and we were still packed standing up but not quite so tightly as before, because four prisoners had died. Of course, there was no possibility of sitting, but one significant advantage was that we could breathe fresh air. The train traveled throughout the night, and I grew cold as the temperature dropped considerably from what it had been during the day. Yet the cold was better than the furnace of pestilence in which I had spent the last four days.

At dawn the following morning, I saw a city water tank with *Berlin* written on it, and I felt better just to know where I was. The train rolled through Berlin without stopping, and I couldn't tell in what direction we were heading. We had been without water for about five days, and all the men were sick. My dysentery was no better, and the odor emerging from me was stultifying. The train continued all day and finally stopped during the night on a siding track. Strong searchlights immediately covered the whole area, making escape impossible. We spent the whole night standing up, blinded by the strong lights. Early in the morning I dozed, only to be awakened by the heavy footsteps of the guards, who paced up and down on each side of the train. After daybreak, a few loaves of bread were thrown at us, enough for all of us to have a few bites; but still we had no water.

In the morning of the sixth day, the train started moving again. The situation in the coal wagon was now as bad as it had been in the cattle wagon. All of us were weaker and were bumping against each other, unable to escape the smell that permeated our rags and our skin. Some of the prisoners complained that they were crushed by the dead men who had fallen against them. At daybreak, the train came to a stop. We wanted to get down so badly that we began to shout, but the guards' only reply was to hit the sides of the wagon.

During the afternoon, the train began moving. After sunset I could make out the words *Stargard In Pommern* on a water tank. We were in Pomerania, in northeastern Prussia. After passing the railroad station, the train backed up and stopped on a siding track, and the guards opened the wagon doors and let us out. A few men remained in the wagon— the dead ones. God bless them. Their torture was over.

I supposed that a prisoner camp was somewhere nearby when we were ordered into line and then counted at least a dozen times. Finally we started walking. My bare feet were still sore and infected, though my hand and neck were better. We went through the city, dreading a hostile reception like the one in Treves. The population gathered quietly on the sidewalks to watch us pass, but the hatred in their composed faces was clear. Parents pointed at us and raised their young children to better see us.

We left the city, and as we walked into the countryside, the object of our thousand-mile trip came into view-a huge camp protected by watchtowers and guard dogs. I was assigned to a barracks in every way similar to that of Treves. I was so exhausted that I fell across the first empty bunk that I saw, but a few seconds later a soldier hit me on the side with his gun and told me to get up. Other soldiers in the barracks gave all the prisoners the same treatment, shouting "Pigs! Pigs!" In less than two minutes we were again outside and in line, where an officer addressed us. He seemed choked with rage, and he spoke French like a native.

"You are worse than pigs," he shouted derisively. "You stink so much that we can smell you a mile away."

Don't you know that you are dirty beyond human dignity? How can you have the audacity to go to bed like that? You are all covered with shit and you don't care. If you do that again you will be shot. You are to be taken to the shower rooms and disinfected."

The Nazi decided to give us a lesson in hygiene by having us run to the showers, which fortunately were close by. We undressed and put our clothes in a pile to be burned. I went into the shower eagerly, not knowing then that many German showers were actually gas chambers. The shower made me feel good. When I walked out, a soldier gave me a blanket to cover myself with. Since it was not cold, the blanket was enough, and I returned to the barracks and went straight to bed. I was starved, but more than that I needed rest. In the night, a soldier got us out of bed for another count, but he was more pleasant and the count went quickly.

At dawn we were counted again, and later on we were sent outside for our soup. After standing in line for more than two hours, we were served a couple of ounces of rancid liquid that I swallowed as quickly as I could. It smelled so bad that I thought of throwing it on the ground, but the soldiers were watching. I was so weak and had lost so much weight that I needed food, though I wondered whether the soup would only aggravate my chronic dysentery.

Since the shower the day before, I had continued wearing my blanket, but that evening we all received clean clothes. I was given a blue coat from the First World War, a pair of gray pants from the Serbian army, and a pair of shoes too big for me and with holes in them. I was happy to have those shoes. Thereafter, except for being counted regularly and going out for our daily soup, we were allowed to rest.

After several days an interrogation began. It took place in a barracks converted for the purpose. In the center of the room a few German officers, all of whom spoke French, were seated behind a large folding table. I had heard a rumor that the best possible situation for a prisoner of war was working on a farm, because there would always be enough to eat and the work was easier. So when one of the officers asked me what my occupation had been before the war, I answered that my father was a farmer with five hundred acres of cultivated land and one hundred fifty cattle and that, since my parents were getting old, they had depended on me for most of the work. The officer took down a few notes as I spoke and that was all. Later on I escaped much suffering because of that lie.

Early the next morning the guards awakened us with the news that we were leaving right away. Standing outside, we were counted repeatedly throughout the morning, and when finally the word was given, we moved out by columns of fifty, about a thousand men in all. I recognized places we had passed twelve days earlier when we had walked to the camp; we were going to the railroad station. The guards pushed us into cattle cars. With far fewer men to a car than before, we were able to move about and sit–a luxury, especially after the hours we had spent standing up in the prison yard.

About an hour after the train left the station, it stopped

just long enough to let a few prisoners get off. These stops recurred frequently until dark, when we stopped for the night. It was quiet, and since there was enough room for me to stretch out, I slept well. At daybreak the train moved on, again stopping frequently to let off prisoners. It looked as though I was going to be one of the last to go. Finally, my turn came, and the door of our wagon was opened.

There was nothing but a tiny country railroad station. We walked for an hour or so until we reached the center of the little town of Henkenhagen. The square was fairly large, dominated by the municipal building and its swastika flag. While we were being lined up in the square, I saw a tall, thin German leaving the municipal building. He was wearing the uniform of the Hitler youth leaders, and as he drew near to us, I saw that his face was hard and repulsive. His name was Ernst Vogel.

He greeted us with a resounding "Heil Hitler," and then addressed us in French.

> Prisoners, never forget that you are the prisoners of the great German Reich. Do not forget at any time that all of Europe has been conquered by it and is now under its dominion. England is falling, and within a few days she also will be dominated by our great Reich. You have nothing to hope for, and there is only one thing that you can do: work with all your heart and soul for the glory of our great Reich. You are doomed to spend the rest of your lives here, and your obligation is to help in every way that you can to make our great Reich's empire the greatest in the world. Tomorrow morning, each one of you will be assigned to a farm in the area. I warn you that any attempt to escape will be severely punished. And don't ever forget that we have exclusive means of teaching you discipline.

Having finished his encouraging speech, Vogel left. I was impressed by the purity of his French; he had to be native. Later I learned that he was an Alsatian who had gone over.

We were sent to a large room on the ground floor of the city hall. It had one barred window and many bunks, each one with a straw mattress. The door could be bolted from the outside, as usual, with a heavy transverse iron bar and a heavy padlock. How could they be so well prepared to receive prisoners? As I lay down in my bunk, I kept thinking about that and the tragic, rapid fall of France. Eventually, despite my lice and flea bites, I drifted into sleep, starving again. We had not been fed or even given a drop of water since we had left the camp three days before.

Before dawn, we were all lined up outside for inspection. Vogel emerged from the municipal building to speak to us again. I learned later that he was the most important man in the area and held several official positions including that of mayor. He announced, "Many farmers around here need a hand. They are here right now and are going to come out and examine you and choose some of you whom they think are good enough to do the work. You are not allowed to say one word. You are expected to remain quiet and let them examine you. Do not forget that any demonstration of hostility will be harshly punished."

When Vogel finished his speech, several farmers came out of the municipal building and began to look us over. One of them walked up to me, felt my arms and my legs, and told me to open my mouth. He put his dirty fingers into my mouth to examine my teeth. That was more than I could take. I jerked my head backward to free my mouth from his dirty fingers and I spat in his face. He wiped his face and shouted as loudly as he could. Instantly a soldier was by my side, beating me with his gun as hard as he could. I fell to the ground and rolled myself into a ball to protect my head. The blows finally stopped, no doubt because the soldier became bored with hitting me. I lay doubled up, aching all over. The soldier must have decided that he wasn't quite through with me, because as I struggled to get up, he gave me a hard boot in the belly.

Vogel, who had watched the whole scene, said, "You don't deserve to be called a pig because you're so bad. Believe me, you will be punished as you deserve. I could have you shot for what you did. But, I'm going to think about it. While waiting for my decision, you're going to be jailed. That is all." He looked at me with a vicious smile and returned to the city hall. The soldier pushed me in the direction of the building. Inside was a hall with four doors. The soldier opened one and shoved me inside. Since it was not yet dawn, I sat motionless on the floor, unable to see until my eyes adjusted to the darkness and I could make out a faint light on the wall near the ceiling. It was a small window. I touched the cold, damp wall and realized that the fresh cement was not quite dry. I felt my way around, hoping to find a chair or perhaps a mattress, but the cell was bare. Just a few minutes later the door opened and, without saying a word, a guard handed me a blanket. I was very glad to have it because my nerves were beginning to shatter, and I suddenly felt overcome with despair and exhaustion. I rolled up in the blanket and fell asleep.

When I woke up, it was not yet daylight. I stood up,

walked a few steps, and then sat down again. There I must have dozed off, because I jumped with a start when I heard the door opening. A soldier pushed me into the hall, where the light was so strong that it blinded me. He took me to another room where a young German in uniform was on duty. As soon as he saw me, the young soldier knocked at a door and beckoned me to enter. Once again I was looking at Vogel, standing behind a table. He greeted me in French. "How are you this morning? I hope you're feeling better. Please have a seat."

He was ready to have his breakfast, which had been brought to him on a tray and placed on the table. The breakfast was a glass of milk, a cup of coffee, and bread and butter. He continued, "I've had you placed downstairs to give you a chance to rest while I decide what to do with you. It seems that you don't want to work for our great Reich. Think about it. If you choose to go and work on a farm, I'll let you go this morning, and in that case I'll share my breakfast with you."

Not only did I despise the idea of doing even easy farm work for the Germans; I did not believe Vogel. I had to think of an excuse that might get me out of my present fix alive. "I do not refuse to work," I said, "but I'm sick and too weak to work."

"Is that so? If you're sick, it's better for you not to eat. I'll have you sent back downstairs right away so you can rest."

As he finished his final words, he got up furiously and looked at me hard with his arrogant, ugly eyes. Then he added, "If you maintain your attitude and continue to laugh at our great Reich, I'll have you sent to one of our correction camps, where they know how to restore failing health. I'm warning you, in those camps the prisoners soon recover from their imaginary illnesses."

The guard, who was standing by the door, pushed me outside the room with his gun, and within two minutes I was back in my dungeon. I have no idea how many hours I spent in solitary confinement, but after a while a soldier opened the door just enough to put in a small, two-ounce bowl of soup. It did not seem to be rancid, though it was mostly hot water. While I drank it, the soldier returned with a bedpan that he left in the corner near the door. After eating, I thought over my situation, and I decided to continue to fight the German officer. The next time he called for me, it was at dinner time, and he had just received his tray of chicken and vegetables.

"I don't have any time to waste with you," he said. "I don't want my meal to get cold. If you're willing to go to work, I'll be happy to share my meal with you. Certainly, you must be hungry."

"I'm not very hungry and I'm sick," I replied. I thought after a taste of solitary confinement that it would be safer for me to state nothing but that simple truth. At this time, if I had chosen to go to work, Vogel would have accused me of having lied to him so as to avoid working for the great Reich—a very serious offense. But he didn't care to believe that I was sick, and my answer hit him like a whip. He jumped up and made a complete turn around the table. Then he stopped in front of me and hit me in the face as hard as he could. "I'm going to have you sent to one of our camps, where you will soon recover from whatever imaginary disease you may have. Meanwhile, you're returning downstairs. You Frenchmen are all alike and worse than pigs. But we have ways to get the best of you—every one of you."

So I was returned to my dungeon and given the daily ration of watery soup. I drank it, wrapped up in my blanket, and lay down exhausted, unable to think any more. The following day, I was brought again to Vogel during his dinner hour. He shouted at me and threatened me with the worst, including Gestapo disciplinary measures. I kept my ground and continued to say that I wanted to work, but was sick. And so back to my hole. This routine lasted for more than two weeks, during which time, with hardly anything to eat, I lost most of my -remaining strength. I could scarcely drag myself around any more, and I was dirty, with a long, uneven, matted beard that bothered me.

Finally, when I was again called to see Vogel during his noon meal, he greeted me with a more controlled voice.

"Sit down," he said. "Are you hungry?" "No, I'm still sick."

He paused for a moment, looked at me, and said, "I do hate to say this, but by now I'm convinced that you have not lied to me during the past two weeks and that you are sick. I have decided to send you to work in a place where you will be well treated and given a chance to recuperate. But at the same time, you have insulted a German farmer, and you have to be punished for such a serious offense. Therefore, I have decided to send you to work at the construction of a prisoners' camp by the beach. If you refuse my offer, I will have no alternative but to leave you in the hands of the Gestapo. Now you may return to your companions."

The guard pushed me outside. The sudden exposure to sunlight made me feel dizzy, and I staggered during the short walk. When I reached my bunk, I collapsed on it in complete exhaustion, pleased that I had won my point with the German. The barracks was deserted, with all the men out on the farms. I was very anxious for them to return, because I had hoped that they would be able to feed me with some smuggled food. Indeed, they improvised a good meal for me, and I slept infinitely better than I had for weeks.

The following morning we were up very early so that the men could be ready when the farmers came for them. As soon as they left, a soldier motioned me to go with him. It was only a few minutes' walk from our barracks to the construction site on the beach along the Baltic Sea. When we reached the place, the soldier let me look around as I pleased until it was daylight.

When the five masons arrived, my guard spoke to one of them and left. They were decent fellows who fed me before my work began. I was their handyman, a job that was light work, and I could stop to rest as often as I pleased. Vogel had told me the truth when he said that I would be well treated. At noon, the masons had a thirty minute lunch break, and they shared their good food with me. At five o'clock the work day was over, and I returned to the barracks, where I rested quietly in bed. My companions did not return from the farms until ten. The assignment was supposed to be punishment, but I felt most fortunate and wished that the punishment would continue until the construction was complete.

My punishment lasted a good three months, in which I had a chance to recuperate. The infection in my feet and the old pains in my back and neck disappeared. One night as I was worrying about what would happen next, a soldier informed me that on the following day I would begin work at the Bauerschule (agricultural school).

At dawn the next morning a soldier took me to the nearby school, which consisted of four large buildings with a red-brick square in the center. In the middle of the square stood a ten-foot high brick monument in the shape of the swastika. The school director, Hermann Toncheid, was waiting for me at the foot of the steps of the main building. He wore a black Nazi uniform and was a member of the Gestapo. He appeared to me the most perfect presentation of a Nazi. He was tall, with blond hair, blue eyes, and a face shaped like the blade of a knife. I mentally named him Grand-Sec (Skinny-Tall). I felt that he was dangerous and that I would have to be careful.

Grand-Sec greeted me in French and spoke with a sadistic smile-the smile I imagined he might have used after pulling a prisoner's eye out with a fork. "Good morning. I want you to know that you will be well treated here as long as you obey me. You have to realize that we Nazis are not barbarians and that you must not believe everything you hear. You see, much of what you hear is propaganda against our great Reich. I want you to eat in the kitchen always. If you do not have enough and still feel hungry, ask for more. Eat all you want. I'll come back for you in a half hour. Heil Hitler."

The director's speech chilled me, because I was beginning to know the Nazis, and he seemed to be the worst I had met so far. I walked into the immense kitchen and sat down. It had two large stoves, which meant that there must be many people to feed. I tried to imagine what kind of work I would be doing when a woman dressed in a brown Nazi uniform brought some food to me without saying a word. Her ugly look convinced me of her loathing for the French.

I could hardly believe that I was so well fed-the same breakfast served to Vogel every morning. I took my time and ate it all. When Grand-See returned, he showed great consideration by asking if I had eaten well and was feeling better. He took me to a house that I assumed was his, and he showed me the little paths and flower beds, which were full of small gravel. Politely, he said, "I think that it does not look nice to have all those pebbles in the yard, and I want you to remove every one of them. I will be very grateful to you for doing this job." I was dumbfounded and could not hide it. "But can I do it? Surely there are thousands and thousands of them. This is stupid!" He quickly dropped his affected attitude. "Stupid or not, do as you are told, or else."

At that he left, but shortly thereafter he returned to bring a little wicker basket. I had no choice but to begin, and so I got on my knees and proceeded to put every tiny pebble I could find into the basket. When the basket was full, I emptied it a short distance from the house while the German watched, unable to hide his enjoyment.

For fourteen hours every day I picked up pebbles for

three weeks, and by the time I finished, not one piece of gravel could be spotted by the human eye. When I went to ask Grand-Sec about my next assignment, he looked at me for a moment and then said, "After a second thought, I have decided that the paths do not took right without the gravel. So tomorrow morning, I want you to put it all back the way it used to be."

I did not even try to hide my indignation. "Vous etes completement dingue" (You are completely nuts). Although he did not understand French well enough to know what I had said, he was smart enough to realize that I had insulted him. "What did you say?" he demanded. "I want you to repeat what you just said." I replied, "I did not really say anything. I was talking to myself." He left in a furor.

The so-called agricultural school had only a few pigs and lambs. It was actually a Nazi training center for boys and girls from ten to eighteen years of age. The youngsters were dangerously fanatic and had the right to sentence to death anyone criticizing Hitler or the party. They could even denounce their parents and have them sent to concentration camps or shot, if they judged it good for the party. I was so wary of them that I never walked to work alone.

I had begun to receive a few packages of cigarettes and preserves from the Red Cross, which raised my morale somewhat. And in spite of the twelve to fourteen hours of daily work, I regained my strength. I continued to be well fed and the work was not demanding. One morning, as I went into the kitchen for breakfast, Grand-Sec was waiting for me. "As soon as you've finished breakfast, I have something special for you to do," he said smugly, as though eager to reveal his secret to me. When I finished, I accompanied him to his home. Next to the house he pointed out a large wrought-iron plate. "This is the cesspool," he said. "Remove the plate and clean it down to the bottom."

I worked two days straight, with a bucket hooked on the end of a long stick. I emptied the bucket into a small two-wheeled wagon pulled by a horse. Then I took the load into a nearby field where I spread the refuse. When I thought I had finished, Grand-Sec fastened a strong rope around my body in order to suspend me from under the arms, and then he put a ladder into the cesspool and handed me a tool to scrape the wall. I told him I did not want to go down. He shouted, "You do as I say or I'll have you sent to a correction camp tomorrow morning. You have one second to make up your mind. The choice is yours." I climbed down the ladder and started cleaning. It was so suffocating down there that I couldn't work more than a minute at a time without coming up to breathe. The director watched from the top of the hole, casually smoking a cigar, until I finished.

Winter was near, and it had already snowed once. One morning I was told to go to Grand-Sec's house to repair a broken shutter on the second floor. The wind was gusty, and I had a difficult time just securing the ladder against the wall. When at last I reached the shutter, a strong wind picked up the ladder, taking me with it. I landed on my back atop a large stone with the ladder over my chest. I tried unsuccessfully to free myself.

Grand-Sec shouted, "All right, you know you're not hurt. Get up." After a moment I was able to get up while he stood by shouting every dirty French word that he knew; yet when I was on my feet, he told me to forget the shutter and take it easy for the day. I went to the stable, where I could rest better. The pain had spread from my back to my whole body by the time I returned to the barracks that night.

Two weeks earlier we had gotten a new guard, a fine young man who appeared to be always disposed to helping us, and as soon as I reached the dorm, I went straight to him and told him about my fall. He listened to everything I had to say before he replied. "Tomorrow morning you will come with me to the military hospital and have a checkup." Incredibly, the following morning he took me to the railroad station and bought two round-trip tickets. During the one-hour trip to the hospital, we rode together in a tourist car.

At the hospital I was immediately sent to the X-ray room, which was equipped with the most modern machines imaginable. An attendant took the X rays and left. A doctor then came in to examine me, and the first thing he did was to get close to me and whisper in French, "Do not fear. I am a doctor and not a Nazi." I had no broken bones, but the fall had left me badly bruised. "You need a good month's rest," the doctor explained. "I'm giving your guard a prescription to take to your employer. If that doesn't work, tell your guard what is happening. He'll keep me posted and I'll do what I can."

Back in the dorm, I went to bed and rested all day, thankful that someone was willing to help. The following morning the young soldier took me to the director and gave him the doctor's note. The director read the note but didn't look pleased. "Very well, " he said acerbically. "The doctor says you need a month's rest. You may have it, but remember-if you don't work, you don't eat." Then he turned to the young soldier and admonished him for having taken me to the doctor without his consent.

For the entire month the Germans did not feed me, but I survived, thanks to several prisoners who smuggled food to me every night. My daily rest and food restored me. After a few days I began to feel better, and by the end of the month I was able to return to work.

On my first day back the director received me with a smile that put me on my guard, and his voice crackled with hatred. "After tomorrow, I won't need you any more, because in winter there's nothing here for you to do. But you won't be without a job. You'll work on the railroad, where the fresh air will be good for your health."

Grand-Sec's tone convinced me that he had not forgiven me the month's rest and that I could expect more trouble. When I returned to my bunk that evening, a letter from Vogel awaited me. It read: "Prisoner, I have been informed that you are shrewdly trying to avoid working and that you are dangerous to our great Reich. This is to inform you that if you continue your little game we will have no alternative but to send you to a discipline center. Let me tell you that they have very effective ways to break down people like you. Meanwhile, in two days you will leave this place and start working on the railroad. If you resist, you will be destroyed. Heil Hitler."

The next night, I was told that my work at the school was over, and on the following morning, a guard put me on a train without telling me where I was going. The train headed east toward Poland; then it stopped, and the guard told me to get down. I was at a tiny rural station in northeastern Germany, close to the Baltic Sea.

When we had walked about an hour, I spotted a small camp, well surrounded with barbed wire and, at that time of day, empty. Before locking me in a bunk room, the guard told me that I would receive my orders later in the evening. I chose a bunk and rested until the prisoners returned, about ten o'clock, appearing exhausted and sick. A soldier followed them in and told me that I had to go to work at five o'clock the next morning.

I was awakened by the noise of iron bars screeching from the outside as the door opened. A soldier came in shouting, "Up, everybody up. And hurry." In less time than it takes to say those words we had to be ready to go. Anyone tagging slightly behind got a hard lick with a gun butt, which this soldier administered with particular skill and eagerness. After a twenty-minute walk we reached the working area.

The work consisted of moving iron rails and piling

them in wagons for shipment. Winter had come and we had no gloves. With a temperature below zero, bare fingers could stick to metal as if glued. The soldiers were ready to shoot if we stopped for a moment. They warmed themselves every fifteen minutes, but we could pause only for a five-minute coffee break at ten o'clock and a ten-minute lunch break at noon. Any prisoner who slowed down for any reason was given a sound beating and deprived of the two breaks and the food.

Each prisoner had his own iron cup for holding food. On my first morning, when I heard the whistle marking the five-minute break, I picked up my cup and joined the line of men who, like me, badly needed their coffee, the first food they received each day. It was not that the coffee was good–it was water more than anything else–but it was hot and we wanted it. Eighty prisoners worked this railroad siding, and it took more than five minutes to serve the hot water to all of us. The first twenty men received theirs, and when the whistle blew, sixty of us were forced back to work without anything. I hoped for more luck at noon, but I was far down the line, and again the whistle blew before I could be served. I desperately tried to imagine that I had eaten.

That first night, when I returned to my bunk, I believed that I would die if I went on with this work. The Nazis had the best machinery available but wanted us to work like human cranes until we all died. As the days went on, the temperature dropped, and the fifteen or sixteen daily hours of work became more painful. Usually I received neither soup nor coffee during the breaks. What saved me was a few monthly packages from the Red Cross.

I conserved the food in them, and each night I had a little something to eat after I reached my bunk.

Winter brought a bitter Nordic cold and made it almost impossible to work. I still wore the clothes I had been given after the disinfection bath following the six day train ride. They were now rags, and my shoes had sprouted new holes. I also wore an old pair of pants and a jacket that were beginning to shred, providing little protection against the strong, piercing wind that blew at us directly from the sea. By January the thermometer read at least twenty-five degrees below zero.

I could hardly use my hands because the skin was cracked and bled much of the time. At night, after we returned to our barracks, each of us retreated into a world of silent suffering. With the glacial cold, the work hours had been reduced to twelve.

One day I felt as though my left foot was beginning to freeze. That night, as soon as I returned to my bunk, I gave my foot a thorough rubbing. After an hour of treatment and not feeling any reaction, I decided to rub it with snow. I opened the window of the barracks, and with an empty food can affixed to a string I brought in enough snow to give my foot a good treatment. There was no problem keeping the snow from melting, since the temperature inside our barracks was below zero and the walls were covered with ice. We had a little brick stove in the center of the room, but we were given only seven twigs a night to make a fire, insufficient to warm up the room. I rubbed my foot with snow until it became red. I tried to rest but slept very little. If my foot was frozen, gangrene would develop and the Nazis would cut off my foot. The following morning, I was up very early to renew the snow treatment, but the foot was still completely numb.

For several days I continued my morning and night snow treatment, but always with the same negative result. One thing gave me hope–my foot had not turned black. Finally, after more than a week my foot began one day to prickle, and on the following morning, it began to feel as if heat and life were penetrating it. Two days later it felt just about normal, and I thanked God for having spared me the gangrene. By April, it was still snowing but wasn't quite so cold. My near-total exhaustion made me think that each day might be my last, and I was very depressed. One morning at daybreak a guard came to me and said, "Pick up your things. You're being transferred."

"Where to?" I asked.

"Get up, get moving," he answered.

We took a passenger train. The Germans in the train gave me dirty looks, but no one spoke. I recognized the countryside I had seen seven months earlier, but I didn't know where I was going. I didn't think that I deserved a correction camp, but one could never tell.

When the train stopped and we got out, I recognized the little rural station and realized that I was going back to Henkenhagen. Recognizing the place made me feel happy, and I hoped I might find some of those who had been so kind to me before I left. At least I knew that the work would be easier than what I had just endured.

Once I reached the camp, I was told to go to work on a farm the following morning. With my hands so infected that I could not even move my thumbs, I prayed to be sent to a farm where I would eat well and my hands would heal. When the prisoners returned from their farm work, I recognized the ones who had fed me during my month-long recuperation from the ladder fall.

It was a morale booster just to be with them again, and that night was the most restful I had had in months.

Early the following morning I was awakened by the familiar screech of the iron bar as the door opened. One of the soldiers came directly to me. "Get up and come with me. You are going to the agricultural school." I was very discouraged, since I wanted to work on a farm like all the other prisoners. I had no choice but to go with the guard and again face Grand-Sec, Hermann Toncheid. He greeted me with a smile. "Good morning. I am happy to see you back with us. I am inclined to believe that your work on the railroad has taught you a good lesson. That railroad work has proved to be a very good school for people like you, and furthermore it puts a trade right in your hands! Now you can be proud of yourself because you have contributed to the victory of our great Reich."

I said nothing, but I gave him such a contemptuous look that he turned abruptly and left. I went to the kitchen as I used to do and found a good breakfast waiting for me. When I finished it, Grand-Seb reappeared and escorted me as far as the stable. "We need a drainage right here for the stable residues," he announced. "It should be about twenty yards long. Start by digging four yards long by two yards wide. Then we will see."

My hands were in such bad shape that it took me a week to complete the job. During the final two days Grand-Sec was clearly growing restless, but I kept on working at a moderate pace without pushing myself. When I finally finished, he examined the hole for a few minutes. "I made a mistake; my calculation is all wrong. The stable residues could not possibly reach this far. So let's forget about it and cover up the hole."

I was so angry that I began to shake. I knew he was testing me, waiting for a word or a hostile gesture to have an excuse to send me to a correction camp. I made up my mind that I would not give him that pleasure. He lingered awhile to see what I was going to do. I went right back to work, filling the hole. It really did not matter whether I dug a hole and refilled it or did something else, just as long as I was at this school. The work was easy and, most important, I ate well.

One day soon after, I was ordered to build a fence for the lambs. Grand-Sec had given me all the details and then decided to help me. As I fastened the posts in the ground, he held them while I hit them with a sledgehammer. As we worked, it occurred to me that all I had to do was deviate my aim and I could smash his brain. Once the idea hit me, it became an obsession. For each stroke on the post, I told myself, "This is going to be the one." Yet, I finally could not do it. The director must have sensed my intention, because he suddenly stood straight up. "I have to go right now. Let's stop this work and continue another day."

As far as I was concerned, the fence might never be completed. In the following days I ate well, did light work around the school, and began to feel restored. One fall morning, as I was working outside, it began to rain so hard that I sought shelter in the cellar. I had been there only a moment when I heard singing coming from the floor above. I couldn't resist climbing the flight of stone stairs to the main floor. The cellar door opened into a long hall lined with doors, each decorated with a swastika. In the center of the hall was a huge, golden mosaic swastika. I walked silently and found the door where the singing was coming from. Opening it a little, I could hardly believe what I saw.

It was a chapel dedicated to Hitler. At one end of the room was a sanctuary containing a picture of Hitler about eighteen feet high, in an elaborately carved wooden frame. On each side of the picture a wrought-iron candelabrum held thick candles about eight feet high. A wrought-iron rail encircled the sanctuary, and on the outside of the rail a procession of boys and girls in Nazi uniforms filed past. They held candles in their right hands as they paused in groups to kneel in front of the picture, bowing their heads in a gesture of adoration while everyone sang.

I was frozen with horror. People had come to accept Hitler as their god, and I was terrified at the implication of such fanaticism. I wanted to stay and watch them go through their worship, but I was obviously at great risk; and so I quickly returned to the cellar.

As the days passed, Grand-Sec continued to find stupid things for me to do. I did my best to satisfy him without ever speaking, so as to deprive him of the chance to find fault with me. I was not up to another winter of railroad work.

One night, when I returned to my bunk, I found one of my friends suffering from intense abdominal pain that appeared to be acute appendicitis. When we told the guard, he responded that he could not care less so long as Pierre was at work in the morning, and that if Pierre was not, he would be reported and sent to a correction camp. By morning Pierre's condition had worsened. The same guard went to his bed and beat him with his gun until he got up. That night when we returned from work, Pierre's condition was dreadful. He was sweating all over and mumbling about his daughter. He kept wiping his face and then brushing the wet hand against his shirt. The guard came to inform us that the following day no one would go to work. "You pigs are full of fleas and lice; therefore, we have decided to disinfect you." He watched Pierre writhing in pain and talking to himself, but his face remained expressionless.

Before he could leave we surrounded him, pleading for help for Pierre; but his answer was final. "That pig is not sick. Tomorrow he will go just like the others." We gave him such threatening looks that he pointed his gun at us and cautiously backed up in the direction of the door. "One move from anyone," he said," and I'll kill five of you."

The following morning at five the guard returned. He went to Pierre's bed and made him get up at the point of his gun. Pierre got on his feet only to fall down, clutching his side. The guard was angry and would not allow any of us to help the sick man. "Get up, pig, or I'll kill you." Pierre finally got back on his feet. He was very pale, and I felt then that he was dying. "Everyone out," said the guard. "Get going."

We had to walk about two miles to reach the cattle train waiting to haul us to the disinfection center, which was about fifty miles away. We carried Pierre the whole way and placed him on the floor of the car. The bouncing and jerking of the train added to his agony. After about two hours, we got off the train. We found a few poles lying around the railroad station, hurriedly improvised a stretcher for Pierre, and began the two-hour walk to the disinfection center.

After an hour or so, we came to a military hospital and instinctively stopped. One of the prisoners asked the guard to take the sick man there for medical attention. The prisoner who asked received a severe beating, and the guard told us that if we did not resume our walk immediately, he would shoot all of us. We had no choice. A little while later I saw that Pierre was quiet and had closed his eyes. We decided to put the stretcher on the ground and give him a few minutes' peaceful rest. We realized then that Pierre had died. The guard came running over to see what was the matter, and when he saw Pierre, he seemed afraid. He pointed his gun at us and made us walk, leaving our friend by the wayside.

A couple of hours later, when we returned from the disinfection showers with clean rags to wear, Pierre's body had already been picked up. That was part of the Nazis' system. Whenever they had dead bodies on their hands, they left them on the side of the road for a truck to pick up. In that way, no one could really tell what they were doing. Yet many times the civilians were aware of the criminal activities (for example, when the Nazis were burning bodies, the smell could be detected miles away). In those cases I believe the terrified civilians chose to appear ignorant rather than die.

That evening, we got together and pledged to kill that Nazi guard if it was ever possible. Of course our pledge was wild and our plans for carrying it out too involved; but since this was war, we knew that no civil authority would ever find us guilty of murder if we fulfilled the pledge. Although I never saw him again, I never forgot the guard's face. Should I meet him one day, I would find it difficult not to honor my promise.

The day after our disinfection I resumed work for Grand-Sec, but my hatred for the Nazis was now so great that I no longer trusted my self-control. I feared saying or doing anything that would get me sent to a correction camp, and I needed something to distract me from the hatred that burned in me like a high fever. I decided to make an escape plan. If I could actually get out of the camp and return unnoticed, perhaps a bigger plan could be devised for more prisoners.

I was more than a thousand miles from the borders of either France or Switzerland, but escape still seemed worth thinking about. I knew that I needed decent civilian clothes, and I knew where to steal some. Grand-Sec had a son of eighteen who was roughly my build. If I was caught inside the house, it would be sure death; but the more I thought of it, the more obsessed I became with my plan to gamble for the chance of freedom. A few days later, my opportunity to get inside the house came unexpectedly.

On that morning I saw Grand-Sec in his Gestapo uniform, leaving the house with his wife, who was dressed up in her best attire. They looked as if they were on their way to Sunday school. The son was still in the house, so I decided to watch and wait. After a few minutes he, too, came out, wearing the Nazi youth uniform, and left on his bicycle. I had to act fast. If he returned and found me in his father's house, he would kill me instantly with the hope of receiving a Nazi decoration. He carried a knife and pistol, presents from the party.

When the boy was out of sight, I entered the house as stealthily as possible. I closed the door behind me and listened for a few minutes. The house was empty. I went down the hall and saw in the living room large pictures of Hitler and Himmler hanging on the walls.

I went into Grand-Sec's bedroom, but I was not interested in his clothes because he was so much taller than I. The next bedroom was the son's. I didn't want to take any of the suits in the closet, because one of them might be too easily missed. As the only prisoner working around the house, I would come under immediate suspicion. Then I saw some suitcases that contained all I needed—a warm pair of navy blue pants and a few sweaters with some holes in them. I took the pants and a gray sweater, put everything back, and was on my way out when I heard someone coming through the front door, I opened the master bedroom door and hid behind the clothes in the closet. I heard someone walk down the hall and open a door while I held my breath. It was the son. Had he returned one minute earlier, he would have caught me. There was a window in the master bedroom, but it faced one of the school buildings, and if I escaped that way, some of the students might spot me. I decided to wait. Soon I heard steps in the hall again and the front door being opened and closed. I began to breathe easier. The son must have returned because he had forgotten something. I eased out of the house and into the stable, where I hid my precious civilian clothes under the straw.

I had the problem then of getting the clothes to my bunk. That evening when I left the school, I put the sweater on under my shirt. The guard checked me as usual and suspected nothing. As for the navy blue pants, I couldn't wear them under my own because mine were light blue and full of holes. I rolled the pants carefully into my jacket, and everything would have passed very easily except that Grand-Sec was close by at the time I left. He came to me and said, "What are you carrying under your arm?" I said, "This is my jacket, don't you see? It's not cold and I don't feel like wearing it. If you want to see it, I will unfold it for you." He looked at me for a moment and then said, "That will not be necessary. You may go."

As soon as I was out of his sight, I took a deep breath. When I reached my camp, one of the prisoners who had been a carpenter made a hole in the ceiling where I could hide the clothes. It was easy to get a cap, since there were several old ones in the stable, and the following day I took one. Most difficult was finding a pair of shoes. The heels of my shoes were gone, and the soles were so worn out that I had to wrap my feet every day with rags, which usually worked their way out of the holes. That would be a giveaway in an escape attempt, and so I got the idea to ask for shoes.

Three mornings later, when Grand-Sec had finished explaining my work for the day, I said, "I want to let you know that my feet are hurting me. Look at them. There is neither heel nor sole left on my shoes. I have to wrap my feet with rags every day, and still they are bleeding all the time. Could you get me a pair of shoes?"

He gave me a questioning look, then replied, "If you ask for shoes once more, I will have you sent to a place where you will have to walk over cut glass until you have no feet left." With that he slapped me hard in the face. Fortunately, I had nothing in my hands; otherwise, I would have killed him with it.

So I would do without shoes. It now meant everything to me to prove that an escape was possible. One night a few days later the sky was so dark that I decided it would be a good time to try. Our guard came at nine o'clock as usual to count us, and as he was about to leave, two of the men staged a fight. The guard reacted very quickly, trying to control the quarrel by beating both of them with his gun. It gave me enough time to retrieve the stolen clothes, slip out through the door, and hide behind the barracks.

A minute later the guard came out. As usual, he locked the door with the iron rod and the padlock. He was grumbling to himself and swearing. After having a few words with the sentries, he left. The sentries walked around the barracks—one to the right, the other to the left—and met about every two minutes.

The barracks was well protected by a fence of electrified barbed wire set to ring an alarm the moment it was touched. Once the alarm was triggered, the soldiers would shoot to kill. I spotted a good place to crawl under the fence and began to dig an opening in the sand, hiding to one side every two minutes to avoid being caught. When the hole seemed big enough, I had about one minute to squirm through and avoid touching the electrified wire. Soon I was on the other side! I hid myself behind a dune for a few moments to calm my nerves, because by now I was shaking. I went back, two minutes at a time, to cover the hole.

I changed out of my prisoner's clothes and I walked away, following the dune, which gave me protection. To avoid meeting the patrols and their dogs, I followed the sea up to the little road that led to the railroad station. Suddenly I saw the shadows of a soldier and a woman; it was too late to back up or hide. As I passed them I lifted my right arm and said a strong "Heil Hitler." The soldier answered me the same way, since it was a compulsory response at all times.

I reached the station and read the timetable. I was nervous, but I couldn't resist finding out how far I could go, though I had no intention of taking the train. With no money and my faulty, accented German, I would have given myself away. It was time for me to return to the barracks.

Most of the return was easy, since I did not meet anyone, but as I got close to the barracks, I suddenly felt myself sinking. I tried to turn back and avoid falling by holding myself in the sand, but the weight of my body was pulling me down. In horror, I realized that I was failing into one of our cesspools. The hole was about seven feet deep and I was already in up to the waist. I panicked because, if I did not manage to climb back out, I would soon be dead. I thrust my nails into the sand with every bit of energy that I had, and little by little I succeeded in pulling myself out of the hole. The stench was overpowering, but fortunately I could still change back into my prisoner's rags, which I had hidden in the sand. I picked them up and went to the sea to wash myself. That helped some, but not enough.

I still had to get back inside without being caught. Near

the door were two barrels that had once been used as latrines. I turned one, with an open end, against the wall and spent the rest of the night hidden in it. Near daybreak I grew nervous. If the guard was late to wake up the prisoners, it would be daylight and I would never be able to get out of my hiding place without being seen. Then I heard him opening the gate. I was right behind him and walked in before he had time to turn on the light. I was standing by the wall when he saw me. He came close. "What are you doing standing there?" He sniffed me and shouted, "Pig!" I told him that I had been sick during the night and didn't make the latrine in time.

Later that morning at the school, I met Grand-Sec on my way to the kitchen. When he smelled me, he told me to clean myself if I wanted to eat. He didn't have to tell me a second time. I went to take a long shower.

That night, the men wanted to know about my adventure. During my story a thin, blond-haired man in his late twenties suddenly interrupted. "Help me. I want to escape. Let's go together." His name was Jean Sabatier. He told me that he had a wife and two children waiting for him at his home in Bordeaux. Jean said that he did not want to live any longer if he couldn't get back to them.

It was necessary to walk at least two hundred miles to get out of Pomerania; being caught in the state would mean immediate death. I was not yet physically strong enough to take the risk, and I told him that, in any event, his best chance for success was in going alone. I suggested that he hide in the attic for a few weeks while an extensive search was made for him. After the Nazis became discouraged, he would have a better chance to escape.

The escape plans would require a good deal of preparation and thought, and we all got busy working on them. It was very good for our morale because it gave us something to live for. A man needed many things before he could leave the prisoner camp, most of which had to be stolen. Food, maps, civilian clothes, a cap, German boots that one of the men got from a Pole in exchange for some Red Cross food–all were collected for the escapee. Each of us stashed a good portion of our Red Cross supply for him to take.

The prisoner who was a carpenter cut an opening in the ceiling big enough for a man to pass through. He did it so skillfully that no one would suspect the ceiling had been touched. The carpenter thought that Jean could make a hole in the roof and slide down on a rope. We started making rope that would be strong enough and long enough for him to slide down in a matter of seconds. Every night each of us brought a few pieces of string. It took almost a month to make the rope, but it was good and strong.

One night when our plans were complete, Jean hid in the attic. We could not leave the ceiling open, since soldiers often came during the night to count us. In the morning we were anxious to see what would happen. Our guard came in to count us, and after the first time, he thought that he had made a mistake and so started again, gradually becoming more irritated. After ten counts, he exploded. "Where is he? If you don't tell me, I am going to kill five of you right here by this building." No one said a word or moved. He took five men and pushed them outside, and we followed. As he took aim we surrounded him. We were ready to kill him and he knew it. All this time the other two sentries had noticed nothing. He ordered us inside, locked the door from the outside, and left to give the alarm.

Twenty minutes later some officers arrived with ten soldiers and six dogs. As a precaution during the night, we had rubbed pepper on everything that our man had touched. Without saying a word, an officer, Vogel, and the soldiers came in with the dogs, and our guard showed them the missing prisoner's bed. The dogs sniffed the bed and began to run around haphazardly. They never even looked up at the ceiling; our trick had apparently discouraged them. The officer, a fanatical SS man, rather short and heavy, watched the dogs. All of a sudden he shouted, "If you are protecting a prisoner who is trying to escape, you are as guilty as he is. If he is not caught by tomorrow, and if you do not tell us how he escaped, I will have ten of you shot." The mayor added, "Before we shoot you, I will take great pleasure in forcing you to talk. I promise you that we have very effective ways to make you talk."

We had twenty-four hours to explain to them Jean's disappearance. They left without another word. Before we left for work, word was passed around that we needed saws, and by that night we had stolen several. Our plan was to saw one iron bar from one of the windows to make it appear that our friend had escaped that way. After the final count of the night, we began to saw the inch-wide bar, using fat to reduce the noise. By cutting only one bar, we could make enough room for our man to have slipped through, because he was slim. We worked all night, stopping every two minutes when sentries passed. Each one of us worked ten minutes at a time. The saw handles had been removed so that we could more easily hide the blades. By early morning the job was finished; the bar was held in place with a tiny shim at bottom. We all went to bed and waited.

At the usual hour, the Nazis entered. The SS officer screamed, "Up, all of you pigs. When and how did that pig escape?" The prisoner who had been assigned to be the barracks leader was obliged to answer all questions. "He sawed an iron bar and escaped through the window." The officer replied, "Show it to me." The leader went to the window and removed the iron bar. The officer said, "Why would he have put the bar back that way? I know. You are the one who did it." The camp leader explained,

"The sentries would have noticed the missing bar, so I asked one of the men to put it back in place. I wanted to give the prisoner a chance. According to the Geneva Convention, any prisoner has the right to an escape if possible. My duty was to give him a chance."

It would have been wiser for our leader to forget about the Geneva Convention. The SS man smashed his face, knocking him to the floor, and stood over him. "When I have you shot, I will not wait for permission from the Geneva Convention." Then he turned to us. "When we catch your friend, I will have his eyes punctured and his tongue cut off. Then I will have him sent to a salt mine where he will push a cart in a circle twenty hours every day for the rest of his life."

Without another word, he left with the soldiers and the dogs. A few minutes later, we were on our way to work. The camp leader was in bad shape, but he told us that his farmer was a good man and would take care of him. He was right. But he was worried about what the SS man had said. Someone suggested that he escape with Jean. He did not like the idea because he was certain that there was little chance to succeed, and he was afraid of the torture he would suffer if caught. After the last count that night, when our guard had left and locked us in, we went to examine the window. The bar had been sealed during the day.

In the following days we prepared the final portion of the escape. After about a month it seemed that everything was ready. The carpenter showed Jean how to make an opening in the roof. Once outside, he would pass under the electric wire as I had done, and then he would be on his own.

One night, we heard him knock twice with his foot to let us know that he was leaving. Soon after, the carpenter went into the attic to reel in the rope and close the hole. I figured that it would take Jean ten minutes to clear the fence, though we waited in silence for a good half hour before deciding that he was in the clear. He promised that if he made it to France, he would send a letter to one of us with these words: "In our next package, we will send you chocolate squares. We hope that you will love them. "

Three months passed with no word from Jean. Then one day, the letter came. At least we had one small victory to cherish. In spite of my little success and Jean's, we made no further escape plans.

A week later the guards told us that a district officer wanted to talk with us in the barracks. The next morning the guard awakened us with his worst gun beating yet.

"Get up and clean this place. Do you want the officer to see how filthy you are?"

The officer arrived wearing a pleasant smile that looked out of place. He was not an SS man, and since he couldn't speak French, an interpreter translated.

> You are all Frenchmen and there are not any Jews among you. You are fortunate; you belong to the new Europe. Within a few days England, France, and all of Europe will be united into the Third Reich. We have decided to give you two months of vacation with your families in France. Afterwards you will join the German army in the Division of French Volunteers, to fight against bolshevism. I have here all the necessary papers. All you have to do is sign them. You are due to leave in eight days.

We were all stunned that he expected us to wear the German uniform and be Nazi slaves. Never! Our silence bound us together. Quickly, a man was called.

"Sign here," said the officer.

"I will not sign anything," answered the prisoner.

"You will be sorry, but we will talk about it later."

All seventy-five of us were called, but no one signed.

The officer lost his sweet smile and spoke to us grimly.

"You have twenty-four hours to make up your minds. I'll be back tomorrow morning. I can have you either shot or sent to a special camp. Do not forget that we have dominated France and we will dominate you."

The following morning, the officer returned and gave the first man a pen, but the prisoner returned to his place without saying a word. The German drew his pistol.

"Sign or I shoot."

"Good, that will make one Frenchman less in the German uniform," answered the prisoner.

When it was over, still no one signed. The officer put the forms back in his briefcase. "This is the way you will have it. In eight days you will be sent to a special camp, and I will make certain that you are treated accordingly."

On the ninth day, ten soldiers walked into the barracks and ordered us to prepare for our departure. It took very little time for each man to gather his belongings. One of the prisoners, who had broken his arm only the day before, was in great pain and could not move as fast as the others. An impatient soldier hit him on his broken arm and the man fell to his knees, stunned from the pain. The soldier continued to hit the broken arm with his gun butt until the prisoner passed out. The soldier then shot him in the chest.

None of us had any way of finding out if the prisoner died instantly, because we were ordered into the yard for counting. Soon after, we headed for the railroad station. There were seventy-four of us. We could have attacked and killed the ten soldiers with great pleasure, but then what? We had no choice but to keep going.

At the station a cattle train waited. All of us, twice as many men as the car could hold, were forced inside, not knowing how long we would be confined. The weather, at least, was cool and we weren't suffocating as we had during the previous train ride. Without delay the train began to move, and traveled until that night, when our car was uncoupled and left on a siding track. Late the next morning I dozed off, but I was jarred awake when our car was hooked to another train, a local one that stopped frequently. We were without food and water.

Finally the train came to a stop and the door of our car was opened. Our first sight was five Nazis in light brown uniform, and behind them were soldiers with machine guns aimed at us. The Nazis were youth leaders, each accompanied by two German shepherds. The youth were even more feared than the Gestapo, for their methods were crueler.

As we left the cattle car, I looked around the station to see if I could locate the name of the place. On one badly painted signboard I could distinguish only a few Polish letters. I eventually learned that the name of the place was Rawa Ruska. Who would ever think of coming to Poland to help us? We knew that the Germans had invaded Poland and that the Nazis were strong, but surely some country would be able to fight back. Maybe Russia would be the one.

During all the time of our captivity we had continued in ignorance of how the war was progressing. We were confused, depressed, and afraid, and in November, 1941, we could not imagine that one month later the United States would become involved in the war. As we walked toward the special camp, my ruminations were broken off by an uproar behind me. One of the prisoners had just killed a soldier by cutting his throat with a knife.

How the prisoner had managed to hide a knife from the Nazis after all the inspection we had been through, no one could guess. Of course, he was shot instantly with his hand still clutching the knife. We knew that he had reached a breaking point and was afraid of special tortures in the new camp. He had wanted to die before reaching the camp, but not without having had the satisfaction of killing one of his enemies. We understood his feelings, but his irrational act was not going to make life easier for us. Sure enough, the soldiers' viciousness quickly increased. They doubled their blows and forced us to run.

About half an hour later the camp came into view. It was surrounded by two rows of electric barbed wire, separated by a distance of about fifteen feet in which there was more barbed wire. No easy escape here. Above the entrance a large sign proclaimed: ARBEIT MACHT FREI (Freedom comes from work). Inside the camp some prisoners were exercising, which I soon learned was to keep them "in shape" for work. There was one soldier for every prisoner, and the orders were simple: sit, roll over, run, sit, and so on. When a man didn't move fast enough, he was bludgeoned. The sequence lasted forty-five minutes. When the soldiers were not satisfied, the prisoner was hung by his wrists for two hours.

The camp was quite large. We were pushed into barracks Number 35. The inside was absolutely empty—nothing but walls and windows with iron bars. I sat on the floor leaning against the wall and saw that it was covered with bedbugs. No one said a word. After a short while, the door was opened and an SS officer in a black uniform came in, accompanied by an interpreter, a Frenchman dressed like an officer, with shining boots. The Frenchman must have done a favor to be so well treated.

"Up, all you pigs," the interpreter ordered. "Don't you know that when an officer comes to address you, you must be on your feet at attention?" I later learned that the officer was Obersturmführer SS Kurt Schumacher. He strutted in front of us.

> A Wehrmacht officer has recommended you to me and begged me to treat you well. I intend to do that. This is your block. You will have neither beds nor blankets as long as I judge it necessary. You will start working tomorrow morning, and I advise you to work joyfully for the glory of the Reich. You will be awakened at 4 A.M. There will be a five-minute break at eleven, a ten-minute break at noon, another five-minute break at four. Work will stop at eleven. Any attempt at escape will be punished with immediate death.

Then with a smile he added, "If any of you should feel sick, don't hesitate to let us know. Here the treatment is free." He was telling us that they would shoot us.

Not long after Schumacher left, the door was opened again, and a basket full of raw potatoes was put inside. We counted the potatoes and found one for each man. We had not had food or water in more than two days. In one corner of the room was a wooden barrel—the latrine. It smelled so bad that two of the prisoners decided to clean it. They asked for the door to be opened. Two soldiers entered and, learning the prisoners' intention, emptied the barrel on the floor.

"We will be back in five minutes," one of them said. "Clean up this mess, or else you will be punished." We had nothing to clean with, and so each of us tore part of his shirt and did the best he could. Five minutes later the soldier returned. He examined the floor and appeared satisfied. "When you are here in your block, you are not allowed to go out for any reason. If any of you tries, he will be shot instantly."

The block room was just big enough for all seventy-three of us to stretch out close together on the floor. A small light hung from the ceiling, and at 4 P.M., when it was getting dark, the light was turned on from an outside control. It was very dim, perhaps twenty-five watts or less, but it was better than complete darkness. At 8 P.M., the light was turned off. There was nothing else to do but wait for our first day of torture. Bedbugs ate me up all night.

About 4 A.M. six soldiers came in shouting for us to get up. Outside, three trucks waited for us, and we were piled into them as quickly as possible. Two guards went with us in each truck. We traveled over a small winding road through the middle of a pine forest until we reached an open-pit mine with so many lights surrounding it that it looked like a sector of daylight amid the darkness. As we walked through the gate, a soldier handed out picks and shovels. While waiting in line, I heard dogs barking. I looked up and saw some brown-shirted officers standing with the dogs and shouting at us to hurry up.

To get into the quarry we had to walk down an incline that was about forty yards long. The floor of the pit was about one thousand feet long and seven hundred feet wide. When I got to the bottom, I looked up and guessed that we were a hundred feet below the surface of the ground. The quarry was shaped like a huge arc opened on one end.

I could barely make out the figures of men climbing along the rock walls. Dozens of searchlights were anchored on wooden platforms just high enough above the ground so that the beams could be angled into our faces. They were so bright that there were few shadows anywhere.

Soldiers ordered us to go to various places as we reached the floor of the mine. I was put in an area where medium-sized rocks were broken with sledgehammers. Minutes later an explosion shook the floor of the mine violently enough for me nearly to lose my balance. A guard immediately ordered me to keep working. A wave of dust rolled across the mine and enveloped us before slowly settling onto the ground. It was not thick enough to choke me, but I tried not to breathe it until it began to disappear. It was quiet again after the explosion, except for the sound of hammers striking rocks.

We had nineteen hours of work ahead of us and just twenty minutes of rest. It was the worst forced labor I had ever heard of. Some of the older men occasionally needed to pause for breath; but this was not permitted, and before the men knew it, soldiers approached with guns pointed at them. Finally, sirens signaled that it was 10 A.M., time for a five-minute rest. They gave us only a cup of water, but we drank it as if it were champagne.

Some of the rocks were breaking too large, according to the Nazis, and so a group of men had to break the larger pieces and carry them to a wheelbarrow that was then emptied into a dump truck. Pushing the wheelbarrow was no easy job on the uneven ground. I felt sorry for the men, but after a few days I found out that the truck drivers, who were not Nazis, were feeding them.

I believe that I survived because I was young and had always been healthy—I was only twenty-three—but some of the older prisoners were less fortunate. One man in his forties had been told to work close to me. We had been given a glass of water at 10 A.M. and, at noon, one slice of bread smeared with a dab of fat. The older man was fatigued, but he managed to move his pick until the 4 P.M. break, all the while talking to himself as if in a state of delirium. A few minutes after we resumed our work, he fell down. A nearby soldier fired a shot to make him get up, but the man did not move. Three other soldiers ran up and began to kick him. One of them turned the prisoner onto his back, meaning to step on his face, but the man was dead. The soldiers were frustrated at having been deprived of such a pleasure, and they picked him up by the arms and legs and threw him into the pit. Later I learned that the Nazis sometimes fed dead prisoners to the dogs to make them more ferocious. We were sick over the death of that man and had all paused for a few moments, but the soldiers goaded us to continue working.

The four soldiers were only a few meters from me. Without thinking of the consequences, I rushed toward one of them with my pick raised, but he turned around quickly and hit me in the ribs with his rifle. I fell from the force of the blow, and one of the other guards stuck the barrel of his rifle on my forehead. "Idiot," he said, "I could kill you, but death would be too sweet; we are going to take you to the camp. The commander will decide what to do with you." Beating me with a stick, he forced me to get up.

The guards put me in a truck and transported me to camp, where I was locked alone in a block. I regretted not having killed the guard, because it seemed that they were about to put an end to my suffering anyway. The door opened and the commander, followed by his dog, entered and spoke to me calmly. "I learned of your assassination attempt and have reserved a place for you in a medical research laboratory where you will be treated according to your conduct. You will leave tomorrow morning, but for the time being you will return to the stone quarry." The interpreter slowly translated the message, and before long, I again found myself with a pick in my hand. A guard with a tommy gun on his hip was near me, holding three German shepherd dogs.

I worked until late in the night—eleven hours without a minute's rest—and then I returned to the camp. My friends were curious to know what had happened, and I informed them of the Nazis' plan for me. I could not understand the meaning of the transfer, though I guessed that ultimately it would lead to my torture and, possibly, my death.

I spent the night without sleep. Very early in the morning one of the guards woke me. I followed him to the back door and went outside. A Mercedes-Benz was waiting. The guard opened the rear door and ordered me to get in. I sat down beside an SS officer who looked at me indifferently, and my apprehension increased. Seated beside the driver in the front was an SS trooper with a machine gun on his knees.

As we pulled away, it was still dark outside. The driver followed a secondary road through the middle of the forest for several miles. The road signs at the intersections meant nothing to me because I was unfamiliar with the area. We had traveled for maybe an hour when suddenly the car turned down a small gravel road. As we approached, I gradually made out faint lights and then finally the shapes of cell blocks. It was a prison camp; the name of the place was Bartoszyce. The car stopped at the gates and a guard walked up to it. "Heil Hitler," he said stiffly. "Show me your papers."

The chauffeur handed them over, and the guard examined them for a few minutes and let us pass. We drove up to a brick building about three or four blocks long. "Get out," said the guard beside me. The guard in the front seat immediately got behind me and pushed me into the building. I entered a hallway painted white, like a hospital. Near the far end of the hallway a green door was opened by two SS women in gray uniforms. The officer who accompanied me went in while I remained on the outside under guard.

After several minutes the door opened and the officer told me to come in. A fat, bald SS colonel wearing gold-rimmed glasses smiled slightly and stood up. "Heil Hitler," he said. "Sit down. I know why you are being punished, but you will see in a couple of days that the punishment is very lax. The propaganda against Germany is malicious. The guards could have killed you and didn't." For the Nazis, unfavorable propaganda was a constant concern. I had heard similar words earlier from the director of the Bauerschule. The SS man continued. "We need help here. That is why the commander of your camp sent you to us. I hope that at the time of your return amongst your friends, you will be thankful for the commander's goodness." Instinctively, I asked him, "What sort of work will I be doing?" Immediately his face contracted and he rose from his chair. "You are not to ask questions, only to do as you are told."

I was taken to a small room that was painted green. A pile of white clothes lay on a small table. "Undress and put on the pants, shirt, and apron," the guard ordered. After dressing, I resembled a hospital orderly. The guard took me down another hallway, knocked on a door, and put his head through a small opening. "The prisoner is here. "

The door opened and an SS woman appeared. She was

about forty years old and wore a dark gray uniform.

On the front of her white bodice was a large red circle with a black swastika in the center. She sternly looked me over from head to toe and said, "Follow me. You will begin work immediately." We walked to the end of a hall and descended a stairway that led to a basement. At the end of another cement corridor, I saw a heavy barred door. I began imagining gruesome possibilities as we arrived in front of this door. She opened it and told me to enter. In a split second, reality came to me, for it was clearly a torture room furnished with all the needed equipment. In the center of the room a doctor was in the process of working over a sleeping man stretched out on an operating table. He was aided by two SS women, one of whom held a notebook. I remained in place, but the SS women told me, "You are here to work. Begin with those buckets under the table. They are full of blood and filth. I will show you where to empty them."

As I went toward the table, I saw that the man seemed to give no sign of life. With a quick glance, I could see his fate. The "doctor" was forcing through the urethra of the penis a red hot needle. His penis was enormous, swollen by this incredible burning. I saw then that the man was breathing weakly, but not one complaint left his lips. It could not be long before he died. I felt my reason staggering.

As I left the room with my buckets, I heard the doctor tell the assistants, "That's enough for today. I'm going to transport him to the intensive care unit and tomorrow we'll see his reaction. Give him a morphine shot." I walked down the hallway bewildered, with the impression of living in a nightmare, until I heard my supervisor's voice order me to empty the buckets. I realized that I was in front of the trash cans on the outside of the building. "Return to the room to clean the medicine cabinets and sweep. I will come back in an hour to show you the work you are to do each day."

Inside the room the doctor was still cleaning some instruments. He was young and blond, with a rugged face–a zealous SS. He paid me no attention as I went to a corner of the room to begin sweeping, near the torture instruments. Chains hung from the ceiling, with iron collars attached to their ends. Nearby was a heavy iron chair with attachments for the wrists, ankles, and head. A little way down was another, somewhat lighter chair with the same attachments. In front of it was a small table containing a paper press and tray filled with different sizes of pliers. In another corner two chains hung from a center axis that could be spread apart when turned by a crank located on the wall. Was it made to tear prisoners to pieces?

While I looked in disbelief, the door opened and two guards pushed in a man wearing rags; he looked about forty years old.

The doctor glanced at him and said to the guard, "Attach him to the table." The man screamed in German, "What do you want to do with me?" From his accent I guessed him to be Polish. The two guards had not yet gotten him to the table when he tried to break away, thin and feeble though he was. The doctor jammed a syringe in his arm and in a minute he collapsed.

Once the guards undressed him and strapped him to the table, they left. Several minutes later the two women I had seen earlier reappeared and approached the table to examine the patient. "What are you going to do?" one asked the doctor. He replied, "I would like to see if repeated electrical charges to the testicles will sterilize him permanently. You will help me," he added, going to a closet. He returned with a wooden plank that held a generator and small electric motor. The generator had two long wires, each with a metal clip and spring. "Attach a clip to each testicle," he said. The woman planted the attachments into the flesh. I watched her face, which contracted with pleasure. She was an image of the perfect sadist.

"When he regains consciousness," the butcher told them, "put the belt of the generator on the motor and turn the rheostat to constantly increase the voltage." While they waited for the man to awaken, I stayed silently in my corner, disgusted and nauseated. After several minutes the man came to and began to use all his strength to try to free himself.

"It is useless to tire yourself," the attendants told him. "You cannot move, and if you continue to try, we have methods to calm you." Beginning to feel the pain in his testicles, the man raised his head, trying to see. "What will you do?" he screamed. "It is my work, not yours," the doctor answered. He then turned to the woman and told her to connect the current. When the power reached the man, he jolted. "Increase the power," said the doctor. The man jolted again and again and his body began to arch and rise from the table. The executioner stopped the current and applied his stethoscope to the heart. "You can increase the power," he continued calmly.

The SS woman in charge of the experiment looked enraptured as her lips parted in a smile. The man's shrieking stopped suddenly, and his body fell again on the table. "Stop," said the doctor. The female SS stopped the current, and the doctor listened to the patient's heartbeat. He was not dead, but he did not react to anything. One of the women took his blood pressure, and the doctor ordered him to be taken away. Two guards entered, took the prisoner by the arms and legs, and carried him outside without bothering to dress him.

I wondered how long I would have to attend these horrors. It was possibly an experiment to see whether I would lose my mind. They then would tell me I had only dreamed these things; or maybe they would brainwash me so that I could never speak of them. But what did they have to fear? They thought of themselves as masters of the world. I was thinking about this as I watched the women leave the room. They seemed sexually excited. I later learned that indeed these horrors did excite them.

When my supervisor returned for me, she ordered me to leave my white uniform in a corner of the room and took me to a cell with a straw mattress on the floor. She handed me something wrapped in paper. "Tomorrow morning a guard will come for you at six o'clock." She left and locked the door. The paper contained bread covered with grease. I stretched out on the mat to eat, and in a few minutes the light was turned off.

The next morning a guard awakened me and led me to a clean, well-equipped kitchen. The cook was a large, strong man, and he sized me up carefully before handing me a cup of watery coffee. When I finished, the guard led me to a room where a large heap of clothes were stored. "Fold all these clothes and arrange them neatly. You have all day to do it." That evening when he came for me, I hadn't finished the assigned chore. In my cell, he threw some bread on my straw mat and left without a word. I felt somewhat calmer since I hadn't had to assist at the tortures all day.

The next day I had just finished my coffee when a female guard came to me. "You are to take food to the sick." She handed me a platter full of black bread slices. I followed her through a section of the building to an immense rectangular room with an intolerable odor that gagged me. All along one side were wire cages about five feet wide, five feet high, and eight feet long. In them, the sick were sleeping on straw mattresses on the floor.

I approached the cages, all with padlocked doors. The guard said, "Begin with the cage on the end and throw two pieces of bread to each of the dogs." I will never forget the vision of these poor people. The experiments had so affected them that they couldn't move about. They had no one to care for them, and they lived in their own wastes.

The room was overheated and the sick were naked, but by the "kindness" of the Nazis, they had been given blankets. I tried not to look at these people, and so I watched my feet while I threw the pieces of bread; but I could hear their groaning. When I had finished, the guard told me that I would have to take them each a bowl of water that night. She led me to the outside of the building and called to another guard. "Watch this prisoner. He has a quarter of an hour to rest."

I could see the concentration camp just behind the building where I had been. It was surrounded by a network of electrified barbed wire and observation posts. In the blocks, the prisoners were packed like rabbits, four or five in wooden beds stacked on top of each other. They had little or nothing to eat. Those who died were pushed by their neighbors to the floors, thus giving the others more room. From those blocks the prisoners were taken to the laboratory for research. Only a weak network of plain barbed wire surrounded the laboratory, and the four guard towers provided surveillance.

How many crimes were committed in that laboratory in the name of research, we will never know. The German capability for cruelty seemed. boundless. I learned later that to amuse themselves, the SS occasionally put prisoners in holes hollowed out vertically so that only their heads were above ground. The guards stood a short distance away and fired rifles and pistols at the heads, using them as targets. Even more cruelly, they would not kill their victims with the first shot; they slightly grazed the heads or walked slowly closer until the gun was right against the victim's head before pulling the trigger. All victims were not killed on the same day. Even as they were dragged out of the target trenches, they were told that they would be brought back the next day. On the first day of the game, some of the prisoners went insane. Others, knowing that they would eventually be killed, preferred a quick death and, when let out of the trenches, rushed onto the electric fences surrounding the camp.

My eyes were fixed on the guard towers when the supervisor arrived and ordered me to go to the operating room. There two SS women were talking to the butcher. Because I had nothing to clean the medicine chests with, I asked one of the women to give me a feather duster. She looked at me in surprise, as if she had never seen me before. "Who do you think you are? What are you doing in here?"

"I work here and I must clean up," I answered as I turned and pointed to the cabinets. "Very well," she said. "I will took for something for you." She came back with a paper towel. "Take this. I couldn't find anything else." I took it from her without speaking and started toward the closets. "Come back here," she said. When I didn't turn around, she ordered me again in a firmer tone, and so I turned to her. "You didn't thank me and I want you to do so; if you don't, we could use you for medical research. Since this table is free, we could use you immediately." I felt chills down my back, and I thanked her. "That's better," she said. "Don't forget it in the future." I turned to my work but felt her eyes fixed on me.

I was cleaning the metal boxes filled with instruments when the door opened and two guards carried in a young woman whose head was shaved. "Undress her," the butcher told them. The two guards smiled and tried to remove her rags, but she fought them. She quickly received a shot and fell to the floor. The guards undressed her, attached metal clamps around her ankles, and suspended her by rings upside down. "Take her blood pressure," the doctor ordered the SS women, "and in an hour unhang her and take her pressure again. If all goes well, hang her up again for three hours. We want to determine how long she can live hanging upside down."

Several seconds later, the woman woke up and fought to get down. One of the SS women approached her. "It's useless to cry out; you will remain suspended as long as I find it necessary." The woman stopped fighting and pleaded feebly, "Kill me now." The doctor replied, "No, my dear. I am going to leave you hanging to see how long it will take you to die. It is an extremely interesting experiment that I will need in the future." The woman was silent and the butcher left the room. I continued to clean the medicine cabinets for an hour or more. When I later looked at the suspended prisoner, her entire head was a purplish blue, her eyes were closed, and her body seemed lifeless.

One of the SS went over to her. "How do you feel?" There was no reply. "Answer me when I talk to you," screamed the SS, slapping the woman with all her strength. From the shock, the woman's head swayed loosely, but she said nothing. "I am going to wake her up," said the SS. She left the room and came back with a pack of cigarettes. She smoked awhile and then put out the cigarette on one of the woman's breasts. The woman pitched forward and opened her eyes. "You see," said the SS. "This little tramp was pretending. Now I know how to wake her up."

A short while later, an SS officer entered and ordered me to go with her. I marched in step with her down a long corridor. We stopped at a door and she told me to go in. It was a tiny room with a grilled window and straw mat on the floor. "You sleep here," she told me.

"Now you may go to the kitchen. The cook will give you something to eat. But don't forget that you are under constant surveillance." On one corner of my mat was a blanket and a bucket; but there was no water, nor a chair. The walls and floor were cement. A small nook in the ceiling held an electric light bulb protected by a metal grillwork.

After receiving my plate of bread in the kitchen, I brought it back to my cell. It was dark inside, but I found the light switch and laid down. I sat up quickly when someone touched the door. A key turned to lock me in for the night. I wasn't hungry but forced myself to eat. If I left food on my plate, the Nazis wouldn't give me any the next day. Sleep, when it finally came, was crowded with nightmares. I would wake up panting and, in the darkness, keep my eyes open for a while.

In the morning I heard the key in the lock and a guard came in and told me to get up. He then turned the light on and left. In the hallway, I saw no one, and so I returned my plate to the kitchen. The cook was there, and he handed me a cup of coffee. While I drank, I looked around the room. A large table was set with ten plates filled with bread, marmalade, margarine, and eggs, and with cups of coffee and milk.

I was staring at the plates when five young SS women that I had never seen before came into the room. They seemed to be between twenty and twenty-five years old. Each wore a tight-fitting white blouse cut low at the neck, a short gray skirt that came to mid-thigh, and black boots. To complete the ensemble, each wore a swastika pendant. Such uniforms were highly unusual. They were a frightening bunch, and their only topic of conversation was torture. I was wondering about them when the cook told me to leave for work.

I descended the stairs, dreading having to go into the butcher's room. I was genuinely afraid of going insane. When I entered, the doctor's back was to me and he was busy preparing his instruments. I saw that the woman who had been suspended upside down the day before was no longer there. The butcher turned around slowly and told me good morning, and I answered with clenched teeth, going toward a medicine chest to busy myself. But he stopped me and said, "Come here. I would like to talk to you." I walked toward him, not knowing what to expect. "You certainly do not approve of our methods," he said. "But nevertheless they have a purpose: to be able to care for our soldiers who contract various kinds of diseases on the Russian front, to preserve the pure German race, and to eliminate all those who resist the Third Reich. Those who want to contribute to the grandeur of Germany will remain alive as slaves—and we have millions. The country will become extremely rich, because this manpower will not be paid, only fed. Can you realize the greatness of the Third Reich in a year or two?" The best I could do was to keep quiet. My words would change nothing.

The door opened and two young SS women came in, dressed in very short skirts and sheer black stockings. I had not seen them in the kitchen. One of them spoke to the doctor. "If you have any patients today, we would be happy to help you. My name is Ruth. Feel free to come for us at any time."

"Agreed," he answered. "I'll call for you."

They left the room laughing as my heart began to pound in anticipation of what I might next have to see. It wasn't long before I knew. Two guards came in, holding up a man who had difficulty walking. He was about forty years old. The man struggled with the guards and swore at them in French. I was ashamed to find myself in the presence of a fellow countryman whom the Nazis were going to torture. According to the butcher's order, he was attached to the small chair by the ankles, a belt was strapped across his stomach, and his wrists were bound to the arm rests, leaving his hands free. The guards left, and the butcher pushed the small table in front of the chair against the man. On the table was a paper press. Ignoring the insults of the prisoner, the doctor went to make a telephone call and quickly returned to him.

A moment later, the two young SS girls came back. "What can we do?" they asked. The doctor replied, "Put the four fingers of his left hand in the press. When you hear each bone break, take out his hand." The girl named Ruth went toward the press, but the man clenched his fist. "Open your hand," she yelled, but the man did not move. "I am going to poke out your eye," she snapped. The doctor intervened. "Not so fast. Leave him in good condition. I'll need him for my experiments on bones." He turned toward the prisoner. "If you don't open your fist, you will doubly suffer." The man did not loosen his grip. "Take his pants off," the doctor ordered. As the girls were detaching the clamps around his ankles, the man kicked Ruth in the face. She fell on her back, stunned, and when she clapped her hand to her mouth, blood ran between her fingers.

The other SS woman opened the door and called for the guards. When they entered, she told them, "Remove his pants, and if he resists, kill him." The prisoner allowed the guards to take off his pants and attach the straps around his ankles. In the meantime the doctor attended to Ruth's mouth, which was beginning to swell. He cleaned her mouth and face with alcohol and put a bandage on her cheek. She was pale and terribly angry. "When you have finished with your experiments, keep him for me," she told the doctor. "Fine. You'll have this room and him for two hours." That prospect clearly lifted her spirits. The doctor returned to the prisoner.

"Open your hand." The hand remained clenched. "Very well. You are going to suffer. Heat the long needle." In a couple of moments the other SS girl returned with a long needle, held with pliers. While she waited, the doctor pulled the prisoner's penis until it hardened. "Now shove the needle in," ordered the doctor. The girl obeyed with a smile. The man jerked and then became limp, and the hot needle went from one side to the other. The odor of burning flesh filled the room. "Leave the needle in. Do not remove it," ordered the doctor.

The prisoner's hands were open and hanging off the arms of the chair. "You see the efficiency of my methods," the doctor said as he placed the man's fingers in the press. Ruth watched the whole scene quietly. She would have her turn soon enough. Her companion began to turn the press. As the blood spurted, I heard a weak crackling.

"Remove the straps," said the doctor, taking the hand from the press. The fingers were dislocated. To stop the bleeding, the girl poured on alcohol and the doctor made an injection into each joint. The other hand was also pressed, but the prisoner neither resisted nor uttered a sound.

"May I wake him?" asked Ruth's friend. The doctor replied, "Wait a minute while I check him." He listened for a moment with his stethoscope. "His heart is still beating." The girl rushed to heat another needle and shortly returned. She pushed it very slowly into the man's penis. He came to, straining pathetically, while the girl continued to push in the needle. When she saw the point of the needle going through, she stopped. "It is done," she said. "Very well," said the doctor. "Do not remove them. They've been sterilized, so there is no chance of infection." The prisoner had fainted and the girl seemed disappointed. "May I put in another needle?" she asked. "No, in two days bring him back to me so that I may see the results of the injections." Then he turned to Ruth. "You will be able to dispose of him as I promised you." The guards carried the man away, and I fought off nausea.

After a few minutes, a guard came in and told me to follow her. We went up to the top floor, where a hallway with doors on either side ran the length of the building. She stopped and said, "Clean all these rooms each morning starting at nine. Make the beds, clean the bathrooms, and empty the trash cans. Then feed the sick before you return to the operating room. In the evening don't forget to give a bowl of water to each patient; then you will eat. In the closet at the end of the hall you will find all the necessary things. "

When she left, I began my task. In the first room I opened the locker for curiosity's sake and saw two black SS uniforms with Hauptmann insignia. I cleaned ten rooms before encountering an occupant—an SS woman, half-nude. As I turned to leave, she stopped me. "Come in and do your work. You'll not disturb me." She was one of the SS guards I had seen that morning in the kitchen. She was wearing only her panties and stockings. "I'll come back after a while," I said. "You are only a slave and you must obey me," she hissed.

I began sweeping the rugs near the clothes closet. She came near me and brushed against me. I understood perfectly her intentions—to arouse my feelings so that I would go to bed with her, which would be my death. I'd be condemned to the operating table, and she would torture me. I continued my work without paying her any attention. She sat on the bed and took off her stockings. I moved into the bathroom, but she said, "Come here." I acted as though I hadn't heard her. She repeated her command, and I went toward her. "Stand directly in front of me." I followed her order. She began sliding off her panties and then she laid down.

"Am I not beautiful enough for you?" I stared at her. "Answer," she said between her teeth. "If you don't, I'll call the guards and tell them you tried to rape me." Sensing the danger, I said to her, "You are very beautiful, but as you said earlier, I am only a slave. I am not a German, nor do I have Aryan blood. And I do not have the right to touch you, which is distressing to me because you are one of the most beautiful women I've ever seen." She sat up.

"You are French, they tell me." I answered yes. "Only the French know how to flatter women, and I would like very much to make love to a Frenchman. It would be a pleasant change from the brutes around here." She stood up and began touching me. "Kiss me. No one will know." I said, "No, you are so beautiful and I am afraid to dirty you." Her face softened. "You are a lover. No one ever spoke to me as you have. When this horrible war is over, come back to see me. I will protect you and you can love me as often as you desire."

Putting her arms around my neck, she kissed my forehead. Her kiss gave me chills of disgust. I thought to myself that if I ever came back, it would be to kill her with my bare hands, not to make love. She then said, "I prefer that you leave the room immediately. We will see each other again later." I rushed into the hall, happy to have left on such a good note with her.

I finished my work in the other rooms and went to the kitchen to find out what time it was. The cook asked, "What are you doing here?" I told him I wanted a cup of coffee. "It's not time," he said, but gave me a cup anyway. He also gave me a piece of buttered bread. "Eat it quickly so nobody will see you." I thanked him and gobbled it down. "Don't tell anyone I gave you the bread," he repeated. "It's okay," I assured him. "I won't tell anyone." I drank my coffee and left. This man, I thought, is surely not a Nazi.

I was on my way to the operating room when a guard called to me. "Go to the kitchen. The cook wants to see you." Back in the kitchen the cook asked, "Have you given water to the sick?" I said that I hadn't yet. "Then do it now," he said. He prepared the bowls, placed them in two baskets, and telephoned for a guard. I followed him into the room where the victims were caged.

The guard opened the first cage, and I was about to put the bowl in the doorway when he said, "No. Place it near his head." In spite of myself I looked at the man and my heart almost stopped. He was half-covered by a blanket. The toenails had been pulled off, and his legs were enormously swollen. His eyes were opened large and he didn't appear to see me. Had they blinded him, too? His breathing was hoarse. I put the bowl on the floor and moved away.

"Hurry up," the guard yelled. "We aren't going to stay in here an hour. These dogs stink." I turned around with the urge to kill him. The guard, understanding, lowered his head and told me to move along. In the second cage was a young woman, about twenty-five years old. The lower half of her body was unmarked. I leaned forward to place the bowl of water, when she sat up and began screaming. Then she began laughing in a frenzy. The cover slipped onto her thighs, and I saw that one of her breasts had been removed; the blood still dripped. Her head had been shaved, and there was a long incision in the scalp. With the back of her hand she hit the bowl and turned it over.

"Get out of there and serve the next," ordered the guard. In the third cage was a man who looked about thirty years old. He sat with difficulty and spoke to me in Russian or Czech. Since I did not understand, he suddenly pulled off his cover and yanked off the dressing between his thighs. His penis and testicles were gone. I put the bowl down and left the cage with my eyes closed, wet with perspiration. "I quit," I said. "Finish this yourself." The guard raised his gun and put it to my chest.

"Continue your work, or I'll shoot." I asked myself if it wouldn't be better to have him kill me than to go on living in these conditions. Compared to these people, I had little to complain about; so I decided to say nothing and to go on. The day would come when I would be free and glad to be alive. I bent over and got another bowl of water.

The occupant of the fourth cage was a man who had not been obviously mutilated, but his head went from side to side constantly, and he kept his hands on his ears. He was leaning against the side of the cage. As I placed the bowl on the ground, his gaze centered on me. Some liquid had run from his ears onto his shoulders. The butcher had burst his eardrums.

In the fifth cage, a young woman sat quietly. Her head had been shaved, but small blond hairs were growing out. I did not want to look at her, but she spoke to me. "Do you understand French?" she asked. I nodded. "I am Jewish," she began.

> Three weeks ago the Nazis threw my mother and father into the furnaces but kept me for experiments. I have waited for death. About two weeks ago, the doctor operated on me. When I awoke I could not close my eyes. My eyelids had been sewn to stay open. The next day, I was held by two SS women while a local anesthetic was applied to my breasts. Since my eyelids were sewn open, I was forced to

watch through a large mirror, which they put across my knees. The doctor cut off both of my breasts.

I did not suffer during the operation, but I fainted anyhow. During my unconsciousness, they had placed a boiling hot potato in my vagina, then crossed my legs. I awoke and tried to get free, but the two SS women held me in position. They advised me that if I fainted again, they would repeat the experiment. Then they released me and removed the potato. I continued crying because of my pain. One of the women left the room and returned from the kitchen with some salt. "if you don't stop your crying immediately, I'll pour this in you. The choice is yours." The doctor made a dressing for my chest, and then they brought me to this cage. I have been here for maybe four or five days—I cannot say for sure. We only have that electric light and I don't know if it's day or night.

Her face was serene and her body relaxed. "Kill me," she pleaded. "I'm no longer waiting for anything." I could not answer. She asked what I was doing there. I answered that I was a French prisoner sent there to be punished for attempting to kill a guard. Suddenly the guard startled me. "That's enough. You've been talking to her for five minutes. If you continue, I'll report you to the Hauptmann."

The next victim was a young woman who must have been given an injection. All over her were abscesses that ran. Her face was so bloated that her eyes couldn't be seen. Her skin was waxy, and her mouth was open. Stooping to give her the bowl, I saw that she was dead. I told the guard and he said that they would have her removed later.

. In the next cage was the man who had received the electric current in his testicles. He leaned against the metal cage, his legs folded and his knees under his chin. He moved constantly, trying to find a position that wouldn't be painful. He looked at me and spoke in German. "Are you in the service of those pigs?" I answered that I was, but only by force, and that I was French. "Shut up!" yelled the guard. "No talking, or I'll kill you both." The man ignored him and added, "These swine think only of torture and murder." The guard grabbed me by the shoulder and pulled me out of the cage. "Shut up!" he screamed again.

The guard pushed me to the next cage where a man about thirty years old was seated on the floor. His arms were above his head, and his wrists were tied to the cage with leather straps. His face revealed his pain. The doctor had put two metal cylinders about three inches long into his penis, and the blood flow had not stopped. The penis was swollen entirely out of proportion, and the skin was tender and purple. The doctor had probably only put the tubes in a few hours earlier. His hands had been tied to keep him from removing the tubes. I supposed that the Nazis wanted to cause gangrene.

As I put the water down, the man spoke to me in a heavy German accent. "Take these out. I can't take the pain." I replied quickly that I could not, but that if it were possible I would. They would have to be cut out. "Silence! Get out!" shouted the guard behind me. I went past the rest of the cages, but they were all empty. "Your work here is done," stated the guard. "Return the baskets to the kitchen."

When I entered the kitchen, the cook pointed to my

plate, and without a word I took it and returned to my cell for the night. My head felt as if it were going to explode with the visions of all the victims. As always, it was hours before I went to sleep.

In the morning I reported to the operating room, where the SS woman who had tried to seduce me stood with a six- or seven-inch-long metal tube in her hand. She recognized me and smiled. In front of her a young woman was hanging by her feet, legs apart. I could see the Star of David on the front of her shirt. The SS woman coated the tube with grease and began to force it into the woman's vagina. When the tube had nearly disappeared, the SS woman left for a minute. She returned with a small container of boiling liquid and, with a spoon, she put this liquid in the tube. The prisoner screamed for several minutes, jolted, and, finally exhausted, became silent.

The SS woman acted surprised. "What is the matter with this bitch?" she muttered, putting the hot container on the woman's pelvic area. There was no reaction. "What must I do?" the SS woman asked the doctor. "Boil an egg, put it in her vagina, and push her legs together. It is a radical method."

She again left the room. When she returned, she had a bowl of boiling water with an egg in it. Taking the forceps, she removed the tube from the woman, who must have begun to hemorrhage internally, because the tube was bloody. The SS woman then slowly pushed the egg in, careful not to break it. She turned the crank on the wall and the girl's legs came together. A rope was tied tightly around her thighs, forcing her legs to stay together. The doctor intervened. "Let her down," he said. The woman fell to the floor and he quickly examined her. "She is dead because you don't know how to work yet. You need more experience." The doctor telephoned and two guards came to remove the body.

The SS woman was pouting because her toy had died. I continued cleaning the medicine chests, arranging the instruments destined for future tortures with the feeling that my fingers were being burned by each one. The doctor tapped me on the shoulder and said, "A guard is waiting outside for you. The commander wants to see you." I felt weak as I followed the guard to the commander. To my knowledge, I had done nothing wrong.

The commander looked at me and smiled. "Sit down." My legs trembled as I sat in the armchair in front of his desk. "I sent for you to ask if you are satisfied with your work assignment and if you have any complaints. I would be happy to hear and correct them." He spoke with a sweetness that put me on my guard. "We don't want to hurt you. On the contrary, we want a doctor to check you to make sure you are healthy." When I remained silent, he lost his tactfulness and ordered me to answer. I said that I had no complaints and was satisfied. "Good. We have no reports against you whatsoever. In a few days you'll be able to return to your friends. That is all. You may go."

Leaving his office I understood why he had called me in—to threaten me with a visit by an SS doctor. He knew that this thought would never leave me day or night, and he was right. Outside in the corridor, I felt panicky. Why should I need a medical checkup? If the doctor could get his hands on me, who would stop him from torturing me? When would it take place? The waiting could drive me crazy.

When I returned to the operating room, the doctor was there alone. I stood still, staring at him, when something in my subconscious told me to kill him. I walked to a cabinet and took out a scalpel. The butcher caught a glimpse of it and quickly asked, "What are you doing with that?" The tone of his voice dispelled my delusion. I held out the scalpel. "This is dirty. What should I do?" He ignored me, and so I replaced the scalpel and left.

I walked down the hall shaking and feeling lightheaded at the thought of what I had almost done. I felt shameful and cowardly because I could not avenge the deaths of so many. In the kitchen the cook offered me some coffee and bread. I thanked him and told him that I appreciated what he was doing for me. He didn't answer, but I could see sadness in his face. I ate quickly and returned reluctantly to the operating room. I felt better now that I had a friend in the building.

An operation was being performed on a male prisoner when I returned to the ward. Metal tubes had been inserted into the penis and the doctor was not able to remove them. The results they were expecting did not seem to occur. The prisoner was then castrated, and he died before the experiment was over. I was ordered to take the waste bucket and empty it. I carried it without looking at it. My head was pounding when I returned with the empty buckets and placed them under the table. I left to go to my cell.

In the morning the guard didn't lead me the usual way to the kitchen, and I began to worry. I was taken to my old supervisor, the woman who was in charge of me the first day I arrived. She spoke coldly. "I have had you brought here to give you a warning. Yesterday you left your work before time, and you did not feed the sick. Nevertheless, I will not report you to the commander. Our experiments may make you sick and indignant, but they will permit the Third Reich to become the most powerful in the world. We are going to impose a mild punishment. You will assist two nurses in an operation. If you get sick or leave the room before the end, I will make a report to the commander, who will in turn make a decision on your future. That is all."

A guard took me to the operating room at once. A young woman was brought in and stripped of her clothing. She was suspended by her ankles, her legs apart, and a mirror was placed in front of her. Her vagina was then sewn shut. The nurses, angry at her cries, heated wires and placed them on her breasts. When pulled, the white hot wires tore the nipples off both breasts. The prisoner cried once more and lurched to one side. "The bitch is dead," cried one of the women.

The sight was more than I could take. I stifled the urge to vomit, and one of the women saw me. "Don't leave the room or we'll report you. Why are you so pale? Because we killed off another Jew? What could this do to you? We are working to better the human race." Stupidly, she then contradicted her own statement by proceeding to tell me of a horrifying practice.

The SS doctors, she said, performed brain operations that rendered prisoners mentally retarded. Their legs were cut off at the knee, and when those wounds had healed, the prisoners were put on the ground and made to move like dogs. To force them to stay in a sitting position, the Nazis whipped them each time they tried to stand. The Nazis took turns during the day training each "dog." When the training period was over, the tongue of the prisoner was cut out and an iron collar placed around his neck. The SS walked him around the camp, giving him orders. The prisoner would be deprived of food for several days. Then a bowl of meat was put in front of him and he was forced to eat using only his mouth. He was trained to do this by having his face shoved in the bowl. In most cases, it took only three or four days to learn. The prisoners could not cry out or complain. They could only grunt, making sounds similar to barking.

The assistant finished her story by telling me that the Nazis were quite proud of their human dogs. While she spoke, the corpse of the girl had been removed, and I was responsible for cleaning up. Afterward, I went to the kitchen to get the plates for the sick. In the basement, I fed the victims without looking at them, but I noticed that two more cages were occupied.

Later, when I returned to the kitchen for my meal, I learned from the cook that he had worked in a small cafe that was not politically oriented. He was accused of being anti-Nazi and was arrested and brought to the camp to serve his sentence as a cook.

After my meal, a guard came to tell me that my job

had been changed. I would no longer be occupied with the sick or in the operating room but would mop all the floors in the building, clean the rooms, and wash clothes. I was relieved but wondered why I was benefitting from special treatment. The tortures and experiments would continue, but I wondered also if what they were now going to do in the operating room was so horrible that it had to be hidden.

That evening the cook was not alone in the kitchen. A young, blonde SS guard was there heating something in an oven. They had a brief encounter about my receiving bread and coffee, and as the guard left, she told the cook a report would be made of the incident. He became frightened, and we agreed that all we could do was pray and hope for the best.

The following morning my guard mentioned to me that word had been received that I wasn't feeling well. She ordered me to take a shower and get into some clean clothes. After the shower, my new job as janitor began. I heard nothing and no one paid me any attention. After mopping the halls, laboratories, and quarters, I went to the laundry room to wash and fold the clothes.

When I went to the kitchen that night for my coffee and bread, the cook told me he had been ordered to stop giving me coffee, but I found that he had managed to slip sausage in with the bread. Ten more days went by without anyone giving me new orders. The longer I stayed away from the operating room, the better I felt. One morning all this changed when a guard took me back to the operating room.

The doctor was not there, but in his place was the woman who had ordered the cook not to give me coffee. She and two aides were working on a woman. She raised her head and said to "Clean all the chests and the room." The woman was attached to a chair. The SS women were in the process of removing parts of her breasts with acid. Acid was applied to pieces of wire and run through each breast. The victim had stopped reacting, which infuriated the SS women. They forced an iron rod into her vagina but did not get any reaction. "It's useless. She has died," said the woman in charge. "Guards, throw this body in the ovens." She snapped an order to me to empty the buckets and clean the room again.

The SS doctor had been an angel compared to this woman. I thought of finding out her name and putting her on my list of those I would return to kill if I could live through the war. After I emptied the buckets and returned to the room, the woman in charge approached me. "I am warning you—if you don't obey my orders, I have ways to make you. You are nothing but a dog, and dogs can be made to listen." I glared at her with as much hatred as she directed toward me. She told me that if I ever looked at her that way again, she'd pull my eyes out. When I turned to walk away, she hit me on one ear. "My patience has its limits," she screamed. "When I talk to you, you are not to turn your back on me. This is the last warning you will receive. Next time I'll put you on the operating table."

The guards appeared with the Frenchman who had kicked the SS girl named Ruth in the face. It had been two weeks since the incident, but I remembered the doctor promising Ruth that she could have the man to herself for two hours. The prisoner looked worse than when I'd seen him two weeks earlier. He was strapped to the operating table. Ruth approached the table smiling demonically. "I'm going to kill you slowly. You are going to pay for your insult."

She began by burning out his eye with a hot metal rod. She then dunked the top half of his body into a vat filled with iced water. Once out of the vat, he was again strapped to the table and an acid-covered wire was wrapped around his testicles. He was brought to a sitting position, and his penis was placed in a paper press. Ruth turned the crank on the press a little at a time until one guard ordered it stopped. "You are going to kill him," he said. "No, I'm going to turn until one side meets the other," she screamed. Slowly the press came together, and the man quickly died. Her eyes glistened with triumph. She motioned for the guards. "Take this body to the dogs; don't throw it in the ovens."

In the hallway next to the kitchen, a guard stopped me and ordered me to follow her. We walked to the commandant's office, where I was told that I would leave the camp on the next day. Once outside the office, I became happy and bewildered, unable to believe that this horrible nightmare was over for me. I went, for the last time, to my cell with my plate. The following day, right outside the door, the Mercedes was waiting to return me under guard to the rock quarry.

My first day back was a Saturday. I was unaccustomed to the hard work, and before the day was over, I felt very weak. During the day, one of the SS officers ordered me to help change a truck tire. When he left, the truck driver spoke to me. "If you want to escape, I'll help you. Monday evening, jump out of the truck that brings you here. You can do it without being seen. Take the cross-road and walk about five hundred yards; I'll wait for you and flash a light to guide you. I'll take you to some friends who will hide you and put you on a fishing boat that goes to Sweden." I could not believe my ears. If it was a trap, that would be the end of me, and how much torture would I then have to suffer? I finally answered, "I cannot accept. You are German, and I cannot take your word that you are telling the truth." He did not insist. Although I felt that I couldn't take a chance, I kept thinking about it for the rest of the day. It made the time go faster.

The following day was Sunday, and I slept until past ten that morning. Shortly after, an interpreter came to see us. "This afternoon at two you will attend the hanging of a Russian prisoner who tried to escape. We want this to be a lesson to all of you." One of the prisoners shouted, "I bet that you Nazis are happy only when you're killing someone." The interpreter grew nervous. "I advise you to shut up, or I'll take your name and report you to the SS officer, who will be happy to make you take back your words."

"By the way, we would like to speak to the SS officer," I said.

"Why do you want to speak to him?"

"We do not need to tell you why."

"I'll inform him of your request."

We prisoners felt such indignation toward this French interpreter that we decided that one day we would try to kill him.

Early that afternoon five soldiers came to take us to the camp's gathering place. Prisoners from different countries were there. I saw many Poles in uniforms that were worse than rags, a good number of Frenchmen, a small number of Englishmen, and others whose nationality I could not determine. Military marches blared from loudspeakers near the SS officer's home, which looked out on the camp's center. A Hitler banner was displayed in front of the door.

When the music stopped, the Russian appeared. He was a pale, blond man, about thirty years old, and his hands were tied behind his back. A small platform had been made for the hanging. As he climbed the steps, I could see him better. He looked very courageous and strong. As the soldier placed the rope around his neck, he spat in his guard's face. The Nazi hit him so violently that the Russian almost died right there, as he lost his balance and the rope began to swing. The soldier caught the rope and tried to hit the Russian again, but the condemned man kicked him in the belly so hard that the soldier folded in half from pain. The prisoner had nothing to lose, and he was taking advantage of his last few minutes of life to repay the Nazis for some of his tortures.

The SS officer who was watching came up and hit the Russian in the face with his stick. The Russian spat in the officer's face. The officer cleaned his face and gave the signal. The rope began to move, but very slowly so that the prisoner could suffer before he died. We could see his body moving at the end of the rope as he fought to breathe. After perhaps two or three minutes he became quiet. I admired that Russian for his courageous death. It was rumored that the Nazis were particularly brutal with Russian and Polish prisoners.

Much to our surprise, when we returned to our block, we found a bucket of drinking water. The SS officer later appeared. "I see that lessons are good for you. Now, you wish to speak to me. What do you have to say?" I spoke for all of us. "We have come to the conclusion that the Wehrmacht officer was right when he told us that we should participate in the new Europe and fight against bolshevism. We are ready to sign the papers." After thinking about it, we had decided that if the Nazis were willing to give us a two-month furlough, we should use that opportunity to escape and join the underground.

"I will inform him of your intention, and when he has answered, I will tell you whether or not he will consider it. Meanwhile, you must continue your punishment here because you rejected his offer when he first presented it. You will stay here as long as I see it is good for you." If we could gain anything by this, we didn't know. The only thing certain was that we were stuck in the mines. But we had another surprise that night; the light was turned on, and a soldier brought us a bucketful of soup. Perhaps the little talk with the SS officer had helped; this was a day off, but we were being fed.

One day during the following week, a plane flew over the quarry, agitating the guards, but nothing else happened. However, that night, when we returned to the block, we found a note written in French on the wall: *Any prisoner caught picking up or holding an enemy leaflet will be shot.* It was signed by the Obersturmfühbrer SS officer of the camp.

We were excited. Something was happening. We had to get hold of one of those papers. They had to be coming from Russia because it was close by and had planes that could easily reach us. We wondered whether the Americans were joining the war. Just to think of it was good for us, since we knew that the Americans believed in freedom. Any time the Germans were nervous it meant good news for us, and I began to gain confidence that someone could subdue them.

This spark of hope improved our morale, though we continued our forced labor. In the camp, things returned to normal. Every day a few prisoners in the other blocks died, but for us, life went grinding on.

Two more weeks passed, and then one afternoon, I saw a Russian plane flying so low that it almost touched the trees. The Germans began to shoot near us to calm us down. The Russian plane dropped thousands of leaflets, a good many within reach, but we couldn't move while the soldiers and their dogs watched us. For more than a half hour we were forbidden to move, gaining an unexpected rest.

When we resumed work, I saw a leaflet close to me and grabbed it. I quickly hid it under a stone and told my companions not to touch the stone until I could retrieve the paper, even if it took a day or two. I could not take it with me that night, because as I had suspected, we underwent a thorough search at eleven, when it was time to return the tools. They didn't find anything, but back at our block another ten soldiers were waiting to examine us a second time. We had to undress again, and again they found nothing. Their anxiety only heightened our eagerness to learn the message on the leaflets.

The following day, I knew that we would not be examined again, since the soldiers had picked up all the leaflets. I waited until dusk, and as I was helping another man move a stone, I recovered my leaflet. I let one of the prisoners know that I had the leaflet in my hand, and he motioned for me to go empty my wheelbarrow. Then he walked a few yards behind me and screamed suddenly, holding his side. When the soldiers came running up to him, he said that he had felt an intense pain but that it had gone and he was feeling well enough to continue working. The diversion gave me the chance to hide the leaflet under my shirt unobserved. Meanwhile, the soldiers shot him dirty looks and watched him work for a while before they returned to their post.

At eleven o'clock we returned the tools without being searched; and when we returned to the block, there were no soldiers waiting for us. After eating, I read the leaflet,

which was written in French and Polish.
> Prisoners, do not abandon hope. The Germans are not as great as they thought. they have not succeeded in taking Moscow and they will never dominate Russia. Within a few months we will overthrow Germany and free you. Then we will turn your executioners over to you for judgment.

We cautiously passed the leaflet around without saying a word. Afterward, I tore it up and each of us swallowed a piece.

After a couple of weeks our morale was again low. On the next Sunday the SS officer came to talk to us. The moment the door opened, the interpreter shouted at us to stand up. The officer came in and announced, "I have some news for you. The Wehrmacht officer is willing to accept your surrender. He will give you the details when you return to your former camp. However, it is my opinion that you have not been punished enough. Therefore, I will keep you here until next Sunday. Nothing will change my decision. If any of you breaks a rule during the week, you will work an additional day at the mine and do a forty-five minute exercise."

One more week seemed like a very long time, but we could endure it. The week passed without incident, and on Saturday we were told to be ready to leave the next day.

At noon the soldiers came, pushed us outside, and made us run to the railroad station. Again packed into a cattle car, we endured two days of being unable to move and without any food, water, or fresh air. Our situation was somewhat bearable only because winter was approaching and it was turning cold, but the starvation and thirst were as bad as before. I will never forget the continual thirst during all the years of my imprisonment.

When we reached the camp at Henkenhagen, I went straight to my bed. My old straw mattress could have used much more straw, but it felt like a million dollars. After a while we began to beg for water, and the guard finally brought us a bucketful. We knew that we wouldn't eat, since we hadn't worked that day.

The following day I didn't mind going to work because I had rested well, and I was on my way to a new place, a large farm located some distance from the school where I had worked under Hermann Toncheid. I was left there with two other companions. We were hoping that during the day we might have a chance to chat a little, helping the time pass more quickly.

The owner, who was waiting for us, spoke to a soldier as he watched us approach. I got the impression that he was mean and that we would need to be careful with him. He took us to a barn where about forty Poles were having breakfast around a long table. They all had the letter P on their jackets. The owner told us to eat all we wanted and then he would tell us about our work. The meal was a feast: oatmeal, bread, and margarine—as much as one wanted—and cafe au lait. Afterward, I was willing to do anything.

We went to a potato field so huge that we could barely see the end of it, and we were given two feed bags to wrap around our knees and a small hook. The man instructed us to start digging and to leave the potatoes in piles for someone to pick up. There were about twenty men to a row. I worked with my two friends, and as we worked, we talked, but without realizing that soldiers were watching us. All of a sudden, a soldier appeared and hit one of my companions so hard that, for a moment, I thought he was dead. If he had been dead, I think I would have killed the soldier with my hook. The other Frenchman and I examined our friend, who didn't seem to have any broken bones, though his back hurt. We both looked at the soldier with undisguised hatred. He ignored us and returned to his observation post with the other soldiers. We worked for a few hours, and it looked as though we had a fairly good deal until our legs began to feel numb. We needed to move about to relieve the cramps caused from the prolonged kneeling; but as soon as we got up, the farmer ran to us, threatening to tell the soldiers if we stopped work before the fifteen minute rest period. In all, potato harvesting proved to be quite a task, but I was willing to sacrifice a great deal in order to continue being fed so well. At the coffee break, each man received portions of bread and bologna with the coffee. At noon we had a half-hour break and a filling meal of sausage and bread. We ate with the Polish workers, but we didn't know their language, and they refused to speak German.

One afternoon, when we had resumed our work, the farmer began to shout. Four of the Poles, who were assigned to bag the potatoes after we had piled them up, had left a few potatoes on the ground. The farmer called the four, took one of them by the arm, and told him to take off his shirt. Two soldiers held him tight while the farmer beat him with the club he always carried. I had never seen so much furious beating. Within a couple of minutes the prisoner collapsed from pain and exhaustion.

The farmer stopped, saying he couldn't go on any more, and he told the soldiers to give the same beating to the other three. The Poles received their beatings in silence. They are a rugged people, and I respect their national pride. After the beating, they were in no condition to work, but they resumed their work as if nothing had happened.

We worked until six o'clock, when it grew dark, but the Poles stayed on to attend to the farm animals, and they slept in the barn. They could move about with some freedom and without a constant guard, but they didn't escape, because they had no place to go. Almost all their families had been deported to unknown places, and their homes had been destroyed.

One morning, as we were going to the barn for breakfast, I recognized one of the men as one whom I had seen at the correction camp the day the Russian was hanged. He was about thirty, but he looked eighty; his hair was

Nightmare Memoir

pure white and his skin was wrinkled. We sat and talked with him in German, for he knew no French. He told us what had happened to him.

> I feel sorry for you for having to work in this place; it is not good. One day last year the farmer decided that I was not working fast enough, so he started to beat me with his club. I thought that he was going to kill me. I managed to get the club out of his hand and began to beat him before the soldiers were aware of the situation. If they had not stopped me, I would have smashed his head. He was badly hurt and spent two weeks in bed. The same day, the mayor sent me off to that correction camp, where I spent three months. (He pointed to his hair.) You see what they did to me.
>
> When I reached the correction camp, I worked at the mine for a few days. Then they put three other Poles and me in a harness, as if we were horses, and made us carry wagons of stone. An SS officer drove the wagon and whipped us to make us walk faster. At night, we were allowed five hours to sleep. For me, they had a special treatment. Four days a week they put me between the two rows of electrified barbed wire, with about seven inches to spare on either side. I was quickly exhausted from the tension of holding myself motionless and from fear of dozing off. After five hours of that torture, they would send me back to the mine, where I was expected to work as if nothing had happened.
>
> In 1939, I had tried to join the Polish army, but they did not accept me because I was flat-footed. I went back to take care of my parents and to work our farm, which was close to Warsaw. I had a sister, fifteen years old, and two brothers, thirteen and eleven. My sweetheart and I were planning to be married. One day the Germans came to our house and took all of us outside. They shot our parents before our eyes. Since then, I have had no news of my sister and brothers. As for my sweetheart, I heard that she and her family were sent to an extermination camp, even though they were not Jews.

The man's face was twisted, and he grew emotional. "I have come back here because I hope to avenge my family. I know that one day they will kill me, but I have nothing to live for except revenge."

Thereafter the man became our friend, and we worked together for three weeks. One day, just before the noon break, we saw the farmer running toward him. "You are committing sabotage against the Reich by leaving potatoes in the ground. You are going back to the correction camp. If three months there were not enough, they will find other ways to teach you." Two soldiers took the Pole by his arms. They stripped off his shirt, and the farmer clubbed him as hard as he could. The Pole took it silently, and when the farmer stopped, the Pole looked calmly at him and said, "Are you finished?" The farmer became enraged. "This afternoon, I will inform the mayor, and you will leave tomorrow for the mines. Return to your work." The farmer had signed a death sentence for the Pole. Nothing further was said, and we returned to our camp.

The next morning we heard what had taken place. During the night, the Pole had killed the farmer and his wife. He cut off the farmer's head, put it in a newspaper, and left it on the mayor's doorstep. He had also set all the buildings on fire, and a few of the cattle died. The Pole had escaped. By the time we got to the farm, the SS soldiers were there with their dogs. The soldiers took us back to the camp and told us that the next morning we would be sent to another farm.

We rested that day, and as was my custom, when I wasn't working, I was worrying. The Nordic winter with its Arctic cold was upon us again. It had been a few weeks since we had returned from the correction camp, but the Wehrmacht officer had not yet spoken to us. As it turned out, we never saw him again. Perhaps he had been sent to the Russian front for having failed to produce our surrender quickly enough. That night, the guard came to count us. We asked him what had happened to the Pole. He hesitated, but then told us that the dogs had tracked the Pole to the sea, where they found his body with knife wounds. He had stabbed himself and thrown himself into the water. Of course, we knew that we couldn't respond, but we were extremely happy with the results. The Nazis were deprived of the pleasure of torturing him further.

Early the next morning three soldiers came for my other two companions and told me that the mayor had not yet decided where to send me. One of them told me that I was to accompany him that day to get some shoes for the prisoners. Shoes—I could hardly believe it. Ever since I had become a prisoner, I had heard rumors that France sent carloads of food, clothes, and shoes for her sons, though we had never received anything. I later learned that for every ten carloads that came from France, the Nazis kept seven for themselves.

The soldier and I took the train to a little town not far away. In the train, a few passengers had given me dirty looks, but in the town, I was not even allowed to walk on the sidewalks. A few women spat; the soldier was amused.

As we walked toward the center of town, we heard some band music, and shortly after, a column of Nazi youths marched down the street in perfect goosestepping synchronicity. I was afraid that if one of them saw me, he would try to kill me. I crouched a little behind a couple of people who were standing as tall as possible to see the parade, and the young people passed without noticing me, to my relief.

The soldier and I moved on, but at the next block he told me to stop. A large crowd had gathered, waiting for something, and when they noticed me, they began to insult me so energetically that the soldier became alarmed. He stood in front of me and faced the crowd with his gun aimed at them. "This man is nothing but a prisoner of war," he explained. "I order all of you to leave him alone. I am responsible for him and no one is to harm him." The crowd quickly lost interest, and I thanked the soldier for defending me. He seemed to be a decent fellow, and the way he looked at me made me suspect that he was grateful for my thanks.

We were about to continue when the crowd began a fresh outcry. At the end of the street, a wagon displaying a woman was moving toward us. The woman's hair had been shaved off, and her hands were tied behind her back. She appeared to be about thirty years old. A rope around her waist lashed her to a post in the wagon, making her immobile. She wore a black robe, and a string around her neck held a square of white that fell on her chest. The red letters on it said: *This German woman made love with a French prisoner.* No wonder I had been treated so belligerently. The Nazis punished any German who mixed with people of the other nationalities, because Hitler did not allow it in his effort to preserve pure German stock. Guilty or not, the woman had been sentenced to twenty years in a special correction camp.

The French prisoner walked behind the wagon with

his arms tied wide open and a rope around his neck that connected to the post in the wagon. The people cursed and threw rocks at both of them. The Frenchman looked wild with suffering and fear; he, too, had been sentenced to twenty years. He would go to a special prisoners' camp, and she would be in a camp reserved for Germans. One was as bad as the other. I eventually learned that in the women's camp female officers ran the show. They had developed such a refined technique that they could remove one eye at a time, chop off ears bit by bit, and even cut off a nose and tongue without killing the victim.

The most sadistic of these women was known as Irma Greese.

She made a collection of skins from human backs. The skin had to be intact, with no blemishes, and thus it was removed very slowly with a scalpel. The prisoner was always shot as soon as the operation was over. Occasionally, the skin was slightly damaged during removal. In that case, it was thrown out and another prisoner was selected to be skinned. Irma Greese used the human skins for lampshades made in her home. She finally paid for her crimes when she was caught and killed.

After the wagon passed, the crowd broke up and we went on to a warehouse. It contained thousands of pairs of shoes, some a little used but most of them new, and every pair had come from the French army. The soldier filled his bag with about fifteen pairs, picking the shoes at random. I mentioned that there were seventy-five prisoners in the camp, but he was unconcerned. "I was given only one bag; I can't take more than it can hold. Those are my orders. I want you to have a pair. How about these?"

He threw a pair at me and had guessed my size closely. The shoes were not new, but they were in very good condition and only one size too large. They would be good for the winter, and if I took care of them, they would last me quite a while. I put them on and the soldier gave me a cigarette. That night the shoes were distributed to those who needed them most—the prisoners who were barefooted.

The following morning a soldier took me to see the mayor. He greeted me with a loud, "Heil Hitler," and when I did not respond he looked displeased. "Within a few months, there will not be anything left of France. She will be a subject of the Reich. We will even forbid you to speak French," he sneered. When I remained silent, he lost patience and demanded a response. I replied, "You may force us to speak German, but we will always feel hatred for you Germans." He knocked me to the floor and kicked me until he was out of breath.

> I have the authority to send you back to the correction camp. If I do, it will be for three months and you will receive special favors. I know your kind. You are stubborn and uncontrollable. In the meantime, I've found a good place for you, working for the butcher. He already has a Pole, but he needs more help. You had better do your best for him, because he despises laziness. He's punished the Pole several times, and he has the authority to punish as he sees fit. I hope that you will spend a quiet winter.

I didn't like his last sentence in particular.

The butcher was a middle-aged man so fat that he looked as wide as he was tall. He had on a fine pair of boots. I dubbed him Gras Double (Super-Fat). He sneered at me and said, "The mayor just informed me by phone that you are hardheaded and rebellious. Follow me. I'll show you the stables and explain the work I expect you to do." He took me to the back of the stalls and explained that by the time of his nine o'clock daily inspection, I was to have attended to all the animals, including two horses, and cleaned his car. If I worked to his satisfaction, I would have a fifteen-minute coffee break. If not, I would have no food for the whole day and would have to do the work over. In the afternoon, I would work in the field until five, when I would return to attend to the animals. I knew that Gras Double, to wear such fine boots and to have that car, possessed considerable authority, and I reminded myself to be careful.

When I opened one of the stable doors, I found myself face-to-face with a Pole who looked deranged. He had watched me coming. "Close the door," he said in broken German. He then addressed me earnestly.

Be very careful with that Gestapo beast. He is worse than the mayor. He barely feeds me and claims that my work is done badly. I have been here six months. One day three months ago, he decided that his car was not clean enough.

> He tied one end of a rope around my neck and the other to the car bumper, and started to drive. I had to run so fast to keep from being killed that I was afraid my heart was going to give up. I was at the point of falling when he stopped. He told me that next time he wouldn't stop. I expect death any day. Until then, I'll help you. That will make our lives a little more pleasant.

By eight, we had cleaned the pigs, the sheep, and the dozen or so cows. We had left the horses and the car for last. At nine, Gras Double came to examine the work. Upon seeing him, the Pole acted out of his mind from fear. "Come and eat," said Gras Double, not bothering with the inspection. At the house, the Pole explained that it was forbidden for prisoners to eat in family kitchens. We would take our meals sitting on two stools in a small utility room. A few dirty towels hung on the wall near a tiny shelf that held a piece of soap and a glass.

An enormous, crabby-looking woman entered and put two plates of bread and fat on the floor. She returned with a pot of coffee and two cups. A strong smell, like burning grease, clung to her. I couldn't escape breathing it in as she bent over to pour the coffee. The handle of the coffeepot looked dainty compared to the bulging flesh on her thick arms. When she raised up and looked arrogantly at me, I saw that her steel-gray eyes were distorted by the gold-rimmed bifocals she wore halfway down the bridge of her nose. Her eyes seemed too small for the size of her head, and every time she blinked it seemed that her eyes were going to pop out of her head. Her coarse, black homemade dress had an uneven hem and large, crudely spaced stitches. She wore cotton stockings and a pair of masculine shoes with thick soles and blunt toes.

Although she had tightly cinched her dark apron, it was impossible to tell where her waist should have been. She ran a hand through her stringy blonde hair, and I noticed that both her cheeks were heavily traced with blood vessels. Wasting no time with us, she walked clumsily back to the kitchen.

The Pole quickly explained that she was the wife and at least as bad as her husband. "She hates cats, but she attracts them with milk. While they are drinking, she puts a rope around their necks and hangs them. The rope works on two pulleys that he installed for her. The poor little animals don't have a chance of defending themselves. It is her favorite pasttime."

After our half-hour break Gras Double came to tell us to get back to work on the car. It was an Auto-Union, a prestigious car used only by important Nazis, Gestapo leaders in the large cities, and army officials. As I was cleaning the back seat, I found a Nazi party badge. Either it accidentally fell from his jacket, or he left it there intentionally to trap us. I hid it in my pocket, thinking that in an escape it could be very helpful. I decided to hide it in the pig dung until I could come up with a suitable place to store it. I was leaving the stable when Gras Double called me.

"What are you doing there?"

"I heard a noise and came to check in case the mother pig had hurt one of the young ones."

He gave me a suspicious look. "Finish cleaning my car."

With those words I knew that he had put the badge in the back seat and that we would be searched. Afterward, Gras Double came to inspect the car. He examined the outside in such minute detail that it was ridiculous, and then he did the same with the inside. He couldn't find a reason to punish us, and in his frustration he ordered us to take off our clothes. The Pole trembled as Gras Double checked our clothes, shoes, and mouths. He found nothing. "One of you is a thief. I'll catch you and punish you so severely you will never forget it."

"What is missing?" I asked.

"What is missing? I'll tell you what is missing. I have lost my party badge in my car."

"If you knew that it was in the car, apparently it wasn't lost. Why didn't you pick it up? The Pole and I have not seen it."

Gras Double looked as though he wanted to kill me, but he turned and left. I should have stayed quiet.

The noon meal was not much, but I could see that the Pole had not been fed like that in weeks. We had boiled potatoes, bread with fat, and coffee. After the meal, Gras Double ordered us to spread manure over the field. I liked the idea, since it gave the Pole and me an additional opportunity to talk. I learned that he had been in the Polish army when the Nazis destroyed the Polish forces. He was made prisoner, and his wife was sent to Danzig. He didn't know if she was still alive.

Late that afternoon we returned to care for the animals, and afterward we went to the utility room to be fed. It was dark by that time, and we could barely see where we were going. A short distance from the utility room, my head bumped against something soft. I backed up to see what I hit. It was a cat that the wife had killed during the afternoon. She had hung the animal by the ears on the clothesline.

Our plates were already on the floor. The Pole ate as though the wretched serving were a banquet. After we'd eaten, Gras Double turned me over to the guard who was there to take me back to camp. One of Hitler's laws forbade prisoners sleeping at their employers' homes. It was a good law for most prisoners, but it didn't apply to the Poles. They had to sleep where they worked and were thus denied the camaraderie of their fellow prisoners.

When I reached my camp that night, I felt as though that first day under Gras Double had lasted for weeks instead of hours. I had already made up my mind to put the badge back in the car. The next morning, the cat was still hanging on the clothesline, its tongue protruding from its mouth. I was puzzled as to why the Germans were so vicious. I knew that many of them had never accepted the Nazi party and were suffering. But so many had been corrupted by the Nazi philosophy. As for the young ones, it was hopeless, since the Nazis had them under absolute control.

When the time came to clean the car, I put the badge under the mat, leaving one of the corners visible. That way, Gras Double could not miss it when he made his inspection. Indeed, he seemed astonished. "Oh! Oh! I knew that I had lost my badge in the car." I could not hide my anger. "If you knew that it was in the car, you had not lost it. Why accuse us of having taken it?" He hit me in the face so hard that I lost my balance and fell. He was much stronger than I. "Watch your words," he snarled.

In the next several weeks the wife hanged more than twenty cats. Our food grew worse, and we had not been served any meat. The Pole coughed too much and lost weight. He complained how cold he was at night sleeping in the stable. I was not much better off, because I had only a thin blanket on my bed and in our camp the walls were white with ice; but at least I was not sick. Day by day I saw him getting worse. One morning just before Christmas, while we were cleaning the animals, he fell on the straw. I tried to help him, but he told me that it was useless, that he couldn't go on anymore. "Don't worry," he said. "They most certainly killed my wife, and now it's my turn to die."

I told him that I was going to go for help. He thanked me and told me not to bother because I wouldn't get any. Nevertheless, I went to the butcher shop. Gras Double was busy selling meat and was dismayed at the sight of me.

"What are you doing here? You know that you're not allowed in here."

"I'm sorry, but the Pole is very sick and I thought I should let you know."

"Is that so! If he is dying, let him die. Now go back to work".

When I returned to the stable, the Pole had not moved. "Are you feeling any better?" I asked. "No," he answered very weakly. "In a few minutes I'll be dead." I rushed to get him some water. He swallowed a few drops, then choked and fell back dead. I left his body where it lay, hoping that Gras Double would soon come. Finally, after two hours, he did.

"Where is that lazy Pole? Why isn't he working? I'm going to teach him that if he cares to eat, he has to work."

"Don't bother. He's dead."

"So, I'll have to get another one of those pigs, after all."

The body was picked up shortly after. That afternoon,

as I worked alone, spreading frozen manure over the field, I kept thinking about the Pole, whose suffering was over. What did I have to live for? I didn't know. Why not stretch out on the frozen field, simply go to sleep, and die? Such an easy ending was much better than enslavement.

I laid down and closed my eyes. How long I was on the snow-covered field I do not know, but when I felt something hot over my face, I woke up. It was the horse. I scratched him on the head. He was an animal, but he let me love him. I brushed him every day, and when I received goodies from the Red Cross, I always brought him something. Most of all, he liked the cookies. When I returned to the barn, Gras Double was waiting for me.

"What kept you so long?"

"I think I caught the flu. I feel miserable. I can't work as fast as I want to."

He was perturbed. "You think you have the flu? Then I'll take you to the doctor right away. We'll see whether you have the flu. But if you're not as sick as you say, I'll have you take an hour of exercise that will teach you not to lie to me any more."

He drove me to the doctor's office, a couple of blocks away. Several patients were waiting to see the doctor, but he asked the receptionist to have me examined right away. She answered that this was impossible and that it might be between one and two hours before the doctor could see me. Gras Double was angry, but he said that he would come back for me in two hours.

The doctor was a kindly man about fifty years old.

When he asked what he could do for me, I replied that I thought I had the flu. He examined me carefully and said, "I don't find anything wrong with you, but I understand you work for the butcher, and so I'm certain that you don't eat well."

I was scared. "The food is not always good, but I don't complain."

"Don't be afraid. I'm not a Nazi. When the butcher comes back for you, I'll tell him that you have the flu and are weakened from lack of food and being overworked. I'll suggest that you receive better nutrition and a week's rest to recuperate."

"He will never allow that," I said.

"I have as much influence as he," said the doctor.

"Have faith in me."

I thanked him and returned to the waiting room. He had risked his life. Shortly after that, Gras Double returned and spent a few minutes with the doctor. He came out of the office fuming and handed me a bottle of pills. "Tomorrow morning stay at your camp. Report for work after three days." He said nothing more, and he took me back to his place.

Since it was so late, I cared for the animals. That night when I returned to the utility room, I had a decent meal. There was oatmeal, potatoes, bread, and sausage. When it was time for me to leave, Gras Double was waiting for me. "I want you to know that if you don't work, you will not eat. You understand that, don't you?" I already knew that too well, but I knew the rest would do me some good.

The next morning, when the guard came to wake everyone, he ignored me. After the men left, I went back to sleep. During the day I ate some food I had from my last Red Cross package and relished my time away from Gras Double.

That night, one of the men returned to the camp limping. He explained that while spreading manure over the field, he had hit his foot with a pitchfork. The foot was red and we were afraid of tetanus. His farmer had told him to talk to our guard, who would take care of him. But the guard said that he had no authority to take the prisoner to the doctor and that he would not take it upon himself to do such a thing. He used the additional excuse that the doctor's office was already closed.

We had some rubbing alcohol and gauze, which I used to clean the wound while some of the prisoners held the man's arms and legs. The poor fellow moaned, but he knew that we were trying to save his life. We bandaged the foot the best we could. The wound was painful and the man slept very little that night. In the morning, the guard refused to do anything for him. The man could not put his shoe on because of the bandage. His farmer told him not to work that day, and he fed him and gave him a slipper to protect his foot.

Inexplicably, Christmas was one of the Nazis' most important holidays, even though they were fanatically anti-Christian and arrested every priest they could find. On Christmas day, they usually worked the prisoners until noon and then gave them food to take back to the camp. That morning, I got up with the others and went to work. At the house, Gras Double was waiting for me and I felt that something was not right. "I hope that you are feeling better," he began. "I cannot stand lazy people around here. If you're sick again, I'll send you to the mayor and he'll take care of you. Although it's Christmas, you'll have to work all day, since you've already had three days of rest." Gras Double must have taken care of the place during those three days.

The day after Christmas was so cold that Gras Double told me not to wash the car, just to clean it inside. I was doing that when I heard some voices near me. I saw two SS officers wearing the black panzer uniform. I continued my work as if I had not seen them. They came up to me and one said, "Get out of that car, fast." When I did not hurry, he snapped, "You had better learn to obey orders. When I say fast, I mean just that. We want to see Hans. Where is he?"

"Hans? Who is he?" I asked.

"He is our father."

"I have no idea."

"And our mother?"

"I do not know. How can I know?"

I could sense that my answers were exasperating them. The other one, who I later learned was named Johann, had remained silent. He had a whip in his boot that he was moving nervously with his hand. Suddenly he put it under my chin to make me raise my head and look at him. "You Frenchmen are nothing but dogs," he scowled. "You don't deserve to be alive. We are going to spend our two weeks' furlough here. During that time, I intend to train you.

Before I leave here, you will be lapping my boots."

I controlled my impulse to curse him, knowing that, otherwise, they would kill me instantly. Johann put the whip back in his boot and turned around, followed by his brother, whose name was Ernst. Gras Double came out to greet them. He had not seen his sons for a long time, but I saw no demonstration of paternal affection. I watched Johann pointing his whip at me and became terrified when Gras Double laughed and nodded his head to approve what his son said.

At noon, I went to the utility room for my lunch, but nothing was there. Johann came in and said, "As long as I'm here, you're not permitted to enter this room. Furthermore, there is no servant here to serve you. If you want to eat, pick up your plate outside." I picked up my plate and went to the barn. I sat by the horse that had awakened me and felt a little comfort in his company. When I offered him a piece of bread, he sniffed it an turned his head away. After a few minutes Johann came for me.

"On your feet and back to work."

"This is the noon half-hour rest," I said. "I believe that I have a few minutes left."

"While I'm here, you have only fifteen minutes. If my father were not here, I would make you work fifteen hours a day and would give you only one meal."

"Fumier" (manure), I replied.

He did not understand. "What did you say?"

"Nothing. "

"I want you to repeat what you just said."

He was preparing to whip me when his father called him to the house. Johann put the whip back into his boot and left.

The following day at noon, I went to the door to pick up my plate but it was not there. It was so cold that instead of waiting for it, I knocked at the kitchen door. The wife opened it just enough to shove the plate out with her foot. It contained nothing but dishwater with tiny pieces of fat and bread floating in it. I took it to the barn to share with the horse. Again, at the odor of the food he turned away, and so I gave it to the pigs.

That afternoon I had almost finished my work in the field when Gras Double and his two sons drove up.

"What are you doing?" he asked.

"I'm spreading the manure as you told me to do."

"But you're almost finished and it's too early to take care of the animals. I want you to accompany my son to the silo and fetch some beets for the cows."

Ernst got out of the car and said, "Let's go. I'll show you where the silos are." As soon as we reached the place, he began to break the frozen soil with a pickax. I couldn't understand why he didn't give me that job, but I wasn't about to ask for it. The broken ground revealed layers of loose, fresh dirt and straw. Ernst threw the beets on the ground behind him while I tossed them into the wagon with a pitchfork. They were in perfect, unfrozen condition. I was busy scooping up the beets when I heard a muffled sound. Ernst had dug too deep and the fresh dirt that was piled around him caved in so that he was almost buried. His father and brother would certainly accuse me of having killed him. I grabbed his feet and began to pull while he tried to push himself out as best he could. I finally got him free and lay him on the ground to check his pulse. When I had cleaned his face and his clothes, he opened his eyes and looked at me.

"Thank you very much. Without your help I would be dead. Why did you save my life?"

"If I had let you die, your brother would have been the first to accuse me of having killed you, and I know what that would have meant for me."

"Then you saved my life to save your own. I can understand that, yet I still thank you. Let's go back home, and I'll explain what you did for me."

When we reached the barn, he hurriedly jumped out of the wagon and signaled his father, and they went into the house. There was no sign of the other brother. A half hour later Ernst returned to the barn and told me to follow him. At the door of the house he invited me in. I hesitated until he repeated the invitation, and then I walked in. He took me to a well-furnished, pleasant room. The walls were hung with large pictures of Hitler, Himmler, and Goebbels.

Gras Double stood waiting for me. "My son has told me how you saved his life, and I want to thank you personally for having done it. We are at war, and we all know that there exists a mutual hatred between Germans and Frenchmen. That is why I am all the more surprised about what you have done. Believe me, you will not be sorry. I will reopen the utility room and get a table so that you can have your meals there."

I thanked him, and as I was about to leave, he offered me a cup of coffee and a pack of cigarettes. His attitude toward me was completely changed, and I hoped that it would continue for the rest of our time together. That night at mealtime I went to the utility room and found the door open. A clean little table set with a good meal awaited me. I was still worried about the other brother, Johann, and I was hoping that perhaps even he would change his attitude. Just as I was finishing my meal, Johann came in. He was more arrogant than ever.

"I hear that you saved my brother's life. I do not believe it. I know that you set up the whole thing."

I was so horrified that I could not think of what to say.

"Admit it."

"Never," I said, "because that's not the truth. I never touched the silo once while your brother was there."

"We shall see." He jammed his whip under my nose. "One day you will admit the truth, and I'll be the one to get it out of you. "

I decided that I'd better talk to Ernst about this at my first opportunity. After all, if I was at Johann's mercy, I didn't have a chance. The following day I saw Ernst as he was about to drive off and asked him if I could speak with him. "Right now, if you wish," he answered. When I explained what had happened, he attempted to reassure me. "Don't worry. I was the one in the silo, and I know what happened. It will be okay."

My doubts remained. As an SS officer, he simply could not be trusted; tomorrow he could change his story and have me arrested. That afternoon, I went to the silo for more beets, and when I returned to the barn, Gras Double was waiting for me. "You will stop working here for a few days and go to help a friend of mine who is sick. He is waiting for a Pole, and as soon as the Pole arrives, you will come back to me." He spoke with a nice tone of voice, and he left me free to work as I pleased. The atmosphere was so much more pleasant, that I thought it was bad luck to be sent to another place.

The next day I was escorted to the new farm. I waited outside until the soldier motioned for me to go in. I walked into the kitchen, which was poorly lighted by a small bulb hanging from the ceiling and suffused with a strong odor of filth. Inside were two women, one about sixty years old and the other about thirty, both wearin plainly dirty dresses. They both got up and greeted me with the "Heil Hitler." I nodded. When the soldier left, the older woman said, "My husband is sick in bed and wants to speak to you. Wait here one moment."

I could not help but notice the disorder. The table was full of dirty dishes, leftovers, and assorted rubbish, and in one corner of the floor, a large pile of garbage had apparently been accumulating for several days. I expected the worst from these people. The daughter looked at me with such fear that I had to speak to her. "You don't have to be afraid of me; I am only a war prisoner." She screamed, "If you dare move, I'll call the police."

At that moment the mother returned to the kitchen. "What is going on?" she asked, looking at me furiously. "If you touch my daughter, I'll have you arrested." I couldn't stop myself from replying, "I would not touch your daughter for anything in the world. She is too dirty." Before I could react, the mother caught up a skillet on the table and hit me on the head. Fortunately, my cap reduced the impact of the shock, but the blow left me dizzy. "I will not give you anything to eat except what I give to the pigs!" she shouted. "Come this way. My husband wants to talk to you."

I followed her through a little hall and into a bedroom. The light was as dim as that in the kitchen, and the smell of dirty linen nauseated me. The man looked emaciated and yellowish, and he wore a mustache in the style of William II. As he spoke, in an unpleasant, high-pitched voice, I saw that all his bottom teeth had gold fillings. "You are to obey my wife and daughter. If you don't do everything they tell you, I'll have you punished by the mayor." I said, "I am willing to work but I need to eat. I don't want the pig mush your wife said she was going to serve me." He raised up on his elbows. "Shut up! You are here to obey. That is all."

I left the room followed by the wife, and in the kitchen I tested the wife's attitude. "Give me some decent food and I'll go to work." She was speechless, and while she was deciding how to react, I added, "Right away." To her own surprise, I believe, she began to heat coffee and milk, and she put a cup on the table with a plate of bread and margarine. I was just as surprised, being served at the table.

After breakfast, I asked her to show me the stables.

Behind the house, at one end of a yard, an animal shelter housed a few cows, sheep, and pigs. A horse stood outside. The woman said that there was also a field, but I told her that I would attend to the animals first. The place was so filthy that I hardly knew where to begin. At ten o'clock I went to ask for some coffee, but when I knocked on the kitchen door, no one answered at first. Just then I found myself face to face with two military police who ordered me to go with them.

The two women in the kitchen acted as if nothing had happened, but they had made up a story against me. One of the MPs pushed me all the way to the car. Once more I was on my way to the city hall to see the mayor.

"So it is you again!" he said in an exasperated tone. "You really insist on being hardheaded."

"I did not do anything. I only asked for some food. I did not want to eat the slush she had prepared for the pigs."

"You are strong-headed and very rebellious."

"The woman has lied to you about me."

"I forbid you to call a German a liar."

He slapped my face and said that he was going to send me to the mill. Further, if he received one more complaint about me, he would have me sent back to the correction camp, this time for three months. The mill was a windmill where ten Poles worked, carrying grain sacks up steep, narrow stairs to the second story. The farmers brought their grain in one-horse wagons and waited in line while all the sacks were unloaded from each wagon.

The MP took me to the foreman of the mill, a tall, hard-looking civilian who carried a bullwhip. "Get to work," he said. "If I'm not satisfied, I know how to make you obey," he added, flashing the whip. I went to a wagon, picked up a sack, and staggered. I managed to hoist it onto my shoulder, and I started to climb. My legs shook, but I got the sack to the storeroom. When I went down to pick up another one, the foreman sneered at me.

I took a second sack and started climbing, but at the top of the stairs, my legs buckled and I let go of the sack. It fell on the stairs but fortunately didn't break. The foreman was instantly by me. "Pick up that sack, right away." I picked it up, put it on my shoulder, and went on. As I stepped out of the storeroom, I almost bumped into the foreman, who was waiting for me. I could smell the stale odor of his mouth. "From now on you will receive five lashes for every sack you drop."

I had carried six more sacks when the bell rang for the noon rest. The foreman distributed the meal—bread and coffee. The Poles were so exhausted that they couldn't even speak to one another. That afternoon, I picked up a sack, but I was so tired I couldn't get it up to my shoulder, and I let it fall. As I stooped to try again, I saw the foreman's boots in front of me. I put the sack down and straightened myself.

"Pig!" he shouted, taking me by the neck and pushing me to the end of the wagon. He took two pieces of rope from his pocket, tied me by the wrists to the two hind posts of the wagon so that my feet were off the ground, and gave me five lashes across the shoulder blades. My arms felt paralyzed and the pain in my back was excruciating. He slowly untied my wrists and let me drop to the ground. "Now up and back to work." I couldn't feel my arms at all and was unable to pick up a sack. "You have thirty seconds to pick up another sack, or I'll start again.

I told myself that before he lashed me again, I would take the whip and kill him with it. I knew that I could count on the Poles to help me. I didn't move. He looked hesitant, perhaps because he had no soldier there to protect him. A few farmers who were waiting stood quietly and watched. The Poles had stopped their work and begun slowly to encircle the foreman. He became uneasy. I stepped closer to him so I wouldn't be overheard by the farmers. "If you complain to the mayor about any of us, you will be dead within the week." He went white and made no response. The Poles resumed their work. The circulation returned to my arms, and I picked up a sack and slowly climbed the stairs. When I went back down, the foreman was still standing in the same place and not speaking. At four, the work had to stop because of the darkness. I thought about what had taken place. If the foreman denounced me, he was taking the chance of being killed by the Poles. They were not interested in protecting their lives, and he knew it.

The following morning, I was sore all over and could hardly move. Everything appeared to be normal at the mill. I carried many sacks upstairs and dropped a few, but the foreman ignored me and only shouted occasionally to work faster. By noon, I was exhausted. The meal and rest period were similar to that of the previous day. Shortly after we resumed work, I picked up a sack, and before getting to the storeroom I put it down by the millstone and sat on it to rest a few minutes. The foreman confronted me with his whip in his hand. "You are taking things easy, stopping your work like this. This is your last day here. Tonight I am going to inform the mayor that you have threatened me, but before I let you go, I am going to educate you."

With that, he started lashing me. I fell down, and he continued whipping me as hard as he could. The Poles watched as though perplexed. I screamed, "He is going to denounce us!" Then they moved to encircle him, and one got hold of his whip. He looked terrified, and when he backed away, his legs hit the block where the millstone was about to pass. He shouted in despair, "I will not denounce you."

Although the Poles hadn't touched him, he made a quick move to escape; but he fell on the block at the very moment the millstone was passing. There was a short crunch; then it continued to turn. One of the Poles stopped the mill and tossed the whip by the dead body. They helped me get up, but I could hardly walk. I had to look normal, though, because the farmers who were outside the door must not know that I had been lashed. If they found out, I would be accused of killing the man. While I was getting back on my feet, one of the Poles told the farmers that there had been an accident, and he asked one of them to get the mayor. I managed to walk in a normal fashion by the time an MP arrived with the mayor.

"What happened?" the mayor asked. One of the Poles answered, "Just as I was coming to the door with a sack, I saw the foreman stumble on the block as the millstone was passing. I rushed to stop the mill, but there was nothing I could do." No one else had seen the accident. "And where were you?" the mayor asked me. "I was climbing the stairs with a sack. I didn't see anything." The mayor went upstairs, examined the scene, and returned within a few minutes. "There will be an investigation about this strange accident. Return to your quarters. Tomorrow you will have a new chief." He was clearly suspicious, but two things were in our favor: the body had not been pushed and it appeared as though the whip had been in his hand. If the foreman was married, though, he might have spoken to his wife about us. One Pole told me that he knew where the foreman lived and that he had never seen a woman in the house.

The following day was January 1, 1943. I got up as usual at 5 A.M. If I had been on a farm, I would have had the afternoon off, but at the mill I had no idea what they would do with us. It was a bitterly cold day. The soldier who accompanied me to the mill stayed there with me for half an hour before taking me back to the camp. Apparently the mill had been temporarily shut down. I went to bed, happy for a chance to rest. Shortly after noon, the men returned from the farms, and we talked of what had taken place at the mill.

On January 2 Gras Double came to get me. I was happy to go back to work for him. During the short ride in his car, he asked me for exact details about the foreman's death. I told him I knew nothing because I hadn't seen what happened. He didn't press me further, and I couldn't tell from his face what he was thinking.

After resuming my duties, I never saw anyone during the day. At mealtimes the wife fed me quite decently, though she continued hanging cats and leaving them on the clothesline for me to see. I never saw the sons again, and I presumed that they had returned to the Russian front.

In February we still had not heard anything about the investigation of the foreman's death. One Sunday afternoon late in the month we returned to the camp before dark. Between our building and the barbed-wire fence was a space of a few yards where we were free to exercise. Suddenly we heard a plane flying at a very low altitude, and we rushed outside to see what was happening. It was discharging leaflets. We waited to catch one. It was a Russian plane, and it circled over us as the other one had done the previous year. Before we could get any leaflets, the soldiers arrived and threatened to shoot us if we touched one.

The plane made a turn and passed over again, flying so low that it seemed almost to touch our heads. The guards kept shouting at us to stay where we were. The ground was frozen and the sand that covered it was very hard, but one of the men covered a leaflet by forcing some sand over it with his feet. The ground was covered with the papers, but the soldiers picked up every one before ordering us back inside the block and locking the door. We hoped to be able to retrieve the covered leaflet through the window later that night.

One of the handles of the latrine barrels had recently been replaced with a strong wire, which I removed. After the light had been turned off for the night, I reached between the iron bars and scratched the sand with the wire near where I thought the flyer was hidden, and finally I snagged it. The flyer was torn but still readable. We camouflaged the three windows with some blankets, and by the light of a match one of the men read it aloud.

> Prisoners, the hour of your rescue is near. The severe Russian winter is digging a grave for the German army . We have pushed them back all along the front, and they are beginning to retreat. Already tens of thousands of them have frozen to death. We have bombed Berlin. When we are closer we will inform you. That will be the time for you to act. Before long, we will send more news to you.

We felt better knowing that the Germans were retreating. Each man swallowed a little piece of the leaflet. The following morning the mayor, looking furious, came to tell us that whoever should pick up or read a leaflet would be shot immediately.

On my way to Gras Double's farm I could think of nothing else but the message. In those days I saw very little of Gras Double. He knew I was doing all the work and he trusted me. That afternoon as I was spreading the manure over the field, I saw a plane coming in my direction, flying very low. As it passed right above, the horse bolted, throwing me from the wagon. I fell on the plow, and a piece of iron penetrated my shoulder. I was glad to see that the horse had returned to the barn and wouldn't have to be chased. Just then the Germans opened fire on the plane. I was walking back toward the barn when I saw Gras Double's car coming for me.

"You are hurt," he called when he got out of the car. After I explained all that had happened, he looked at me and said sarcastically, "That is what you can expect from the Communists." I supposed that he wanted me to bite on his remark, but I kept silent. He took me to his home, cleaned my wound, and treated it as best he could before he sent me to the camp with orders that I be taken to the military hospital in the morning.

The following day, a soldier took me to the train station. While we were waiting to leave for the hospital, a long cattle train with enormous red crosses painted on it came through, bringing back wounded German soldiers from Russia. Every car was packed with men, and more wounded were fastened on the top and sides of the cars. The civilians who watched didn't move or speak. I wondered what they thought about the promises that the German army would take Russia in one month. The pleasure and excitement of the early war days were over for the Germans. I must have been the only one to rejoice at the unhappy sight of the convoy; my guard was obviously disturbed. The train didn't stop but kept on its way to the military hospital.

Upon our arrival at the hospital, I saw patients stretched all around the walls outside the building, lying in the temperature of just below zero. Inside, the wounded occupied every available space, stretched on the floor, sitting down, or standing against walls. The only way we could go down the hall was to step over them. The doctor I was supposed to see was on the second floor. When we finally reached the stairs, there were so many wounded that it was impossible to get through. The soldier took me back to the entrance and told me to wait for him. While he was gone, I looked at the soldiers who a few months earlier had conquest in their minds. Now there was little left of them but rags—the beginning of the fall of the Third Reich. The soldier returned and told me there was no doctor available. "I can understand," I said, looking at all the wounded.

When we returned to camp, I asked him if he would let Gras Double know what had happened and ask him if I could go to the town doctor. He promised that he would. As the soldier left, I couldn't resist wondering what would become of him if Germany lost. If the Russians came, what would they do to him? He could not expect sympathy from the French. It seemed to me that he knew it already. When my companions returned to camp that night, I told them everything that I had seen during the day, and our morale soared as never before.

In the morning, the soldier took me to the town doctor who had been so kind to me. When he saw me, he asked how I was feeling. "Much better than the first time I was here because now I eat much better." He said, "You have a very bad wound. I'll give you a tetanus shot. How did this happen?" When I told him, he looked around to make certain that no one was watching; then he bent over and spoke close to my ear. "Germany is lost; it is in chaos! We will be completely subdued very soon. I will have to get away from here before the enemy takes over; otherwise I will be shot like all the others, although I am not a Nazi."

I was struck that a German would speak so openly to me. He did what he could for my shoulder and before finishing the bandage, he lowered his voice again. "The Nazis are watching me every minute; they are suspicious of me. It is possible that I may not be able to leave at all. If you are still here when the Russians come, think of what I am telling you today." I looked at him and wondered if he was sincere. He brought me back to the waiting room, and after the traditional Heil Hitler, he told the soldier to bring me back in two days.

The soldier returned me to Gras Double. I could move my arm enough to do light work. The next day I was busy with the animals when Gras Double came to the barn with two Poles. "Your work is finished here," he said. "You're not well enough to do all there is to do. The mayor will find another place for you. I've hired these two Poles to replace you." He turned to the Poles. "The Frenchman will explain to you what you are supposed to do. You had better work hard because I cannot tolerate laziness." I recalled the Pole who had died in the barn the year before and really felt sorry for these two. Life would not be pleasant for them. I was depressed that night when I returned to the camp.

The following morning, a soldier told me to go to the mayor's office. The mayor was waiting for me with a little man of about forty standing beside him. He had an angular face with glasses, and he wore a Gestapo uniform. "This is the Frenchman," said the mayor. The Gestapo man did not answer but came close to me and smiled in a nasty way. "I wish to ask you a few questions concerning the accident that happened while you were working at the windmill." I waited for his questions and tried to look impassive.

"I know that the foreman had lashed you with his whip," the man said. "Can you deny that?"

"No," I answered. "The first day I received five lashes because I was exhausted and dropped a sack."

"But later he punished you again."

"No, that was the only time." He held back for a moment and then shouted in my face, "You are lying. He lashed you again, and to avenge yourself you pushed him under the millstone."

"No, that is not right. He hit me only once. At the time of the accident, I was on the stairs bringing up a sack."

"If you continue to lie, you are going to witness a little scene that will open your mouth and sharpen your tongue."

He returned to the desk and talked with the mayor in a low voice. They had taken so much time to conduct the investigation that I had believed the accident was forgotten. Now they were reviving it. After a few minutes the mayor pushed a button and an SS soldier appeared at the door. "Bring in the Pole," said the Gestapo agent.

I was well aware of their style of investigation. They tortured the Poles to make them talk. A few minutes later two SS soldiers dragged in a Pole by the arms and let him fall in front of the desk. He looked almost dead and he did not move. His face was nothing but pulpy flesh, and they had pulled out his nails and crushed his fingers. He was naked to the waist; his breasts had been burned and were bleeding.

The Gestapo man came over to me again. "This is the man who informed us of your crime."

"It is not true. I received five lashes and no more."

"I am going to make him talk right here before you. You'll hear it for yourself. If he repeats what he has already said, I will have you shot."

An SS soldier sat the Pole on a wooden chair. The

Gestapo agent motioned with a hand, and one of the SS soldiers disappeared and returned almost immediately with a hot steel rod. "Wake him up," said the Gestapo agent. The soldier put the iron on the forehead of the Pole who screamed in agony as the odor of burning flesh filled the room. Two soldiers held the Pole's head in my direction. "Look at him," ordered the Gestapo agent. "Is he the one who killed the foreman of the mill?" The Pole looked at me a few seconds. His death was very close, yet he had the courage to shake his head. The two soldiers were so furious that they let him fall on the floor, and the Gestapo agent shouted. "I am going to make him talk. Bring another rod to me. He is going to talk. I am going to puncture one of his eyes." He got close to the Pole, pulled his head backward, pointed the rod at the eye, then let the head fall forward again. "The pig. He is dead." The two SS soldiers pulled the Pole out of the room, and the agent came back to me.

"I could make you talk by puncturing one of your eyes, but I am not going to do it. After all, we are not tyrants. I do not like to use such methods. Now, tell me who killed that man."

"No one killed him, and he did not touch me. If he had lashed me, as you say, I would have been too sore to walk. The mayor reached the scene of the accident less than a half an hour later. He saw me then and spoke to me. Why don't you ask the farmers who were there? They saw me go up with my sack and then come back down." I was convinced that none of the farmers could remember in exact detail what had taken place two months before.

The Gestapo agent returned to the desk to speak with

the mayor; then the mayor came over to me. "Consider yourself very lucky. If I were not here, you would be tortured exactly as the Pole had been. I believe that you did not kill the man, but I also believe you are not telling the whole truth and that you are trying to protect the Poles. Because of that, I have decided to send you back to the correction camp. You know the place; you have been there before. You will leave tomorrow morning."

He dismissed me and I found my guard by the door. He was as white as a sheet. He had witnessed the torture inflicted on the Pole. While the guard was taking me back to the camp, I suddenly realized how narrowly I had escaped torture. I began to shiver all over, and for a couple of minutes I could hardly walk.

When morning came, I left my friends, fearful of the month ahead. At the railroad station, I met the Poles who had been at the mill at the time of the accident. We were all going to the same place, but they had been sentenced for two months. It was for me that they would have to suffer at the camp, and the thought of that depressed me even more. While waiting for the train, we didn't speak about the incident. Since there were only eleven prisoners going to the camp, they put us in a third-class train. Being seated made the trip less difficult, though we were not fed.

After twenty-four hours we reached the station, but this time there were no brown shirts, no dogs. Once at the camp, we were separated, the Poles sent to a building especially reserved for them, and I to blockhouse number 98. A soldier opened the door and left me inside by myself. There were beds in this blockhouse, but no mattresses or blankets. The prisoners had to sleep on the wood, but it was better than cement. The cold was still very severe and the snow was deep. Inside the building the walls were shining with ice. I walked around and stretched out on one of the beds, but within a few minutes I felt frozen. I knew I had better not get sick if I wanted to stay alive.

I had been in the building perhaps an hour when the

SS officer arrived, accompanied by the same French interpreter who had been there the year before and who still followed the officer like a dog. As the officer opened the door to come in, he shouted, "On your feet. I see your last stay here has not taught you enough lessons. Well, I love to take special care of those who come here for repeat visits." He sneered at me. "Those who come here for a third time rarely leave this place. During the month you should learn your lesson. You will get up at 4 A.M. The count will be done in the yard. At noon you will have a five-minute break and be given one piece of bread. At 5 P.M. there will be another five-minute rest, and the work will stop at ten. Tomorrow you will start working at a metallurgy factory that has been bombed and needs to be repaired as soon as possible. I will punish any infractions when you return at night."

By the time he left I was desperately cold. I didn't know what to do with myself, and so I decided to walk, hoping that exercise would warm me, but nothing could. Late that afternoon it was as dark as in the middle of the night, and I couldn't turn on the light because it was controlled by a central system. I tried to sleep but was too cold. At ten the light came on, a low-watt bulb that hung from the ceiling and left most of the place still in obscurity.

About ten-thirty I heard the trucks stop outside, and a minute later the men—all French—came in. They paid me no attention; all they wanted was to stretch out on their boards and try to get some rest. A few minutes later two soldiers brought the soup and a bucket of water.

Many of the men were so tired they didn't even get up for it. The soup was the same glue that I had eaten here before, a meal that even a famished dog might have refused; but I took some, hoping that it would help me fight the cold. One man asked me how much time I would have to spend there. I told him one month, and he replied that one month was nothing. He would be there for three months and still had a month and a half to go.

At 4 A.M. we had to get up. I hadn't been able to sleep because it was too cold even to doze off. It had snowed very heavily during the night, and it was bitterly cold. Outside the guard lined us up to be counted, and then left. Ten, fifteen, twenty minutes passed. What were they waiting for? There we were, standing in formation in the snow, waiting to be counted, and no one came. One of the men finally enlightened me. "The sergeant will not count us until six. They leave us here for two hours. They say we need to be trained."

The sergeant, a small, fat man, finally came, holding a flashlight in one hand and a whip in the other. Some of the men were so tired that they were sleeping while standing, supported by the men next to them. The sergeant looked at us from the end of the two rows of men and shouted, "Straighten yourselves. If not, I will have you do forty-five minutes of exercise before you go to work."

Before the count began, he examined us for fifteen minutes with his flashlight, lifting our heads, one by one, with his whip. After the examination, he counted us a number of times and finally gave the order to go. After two hours of fighting against cold, snow, and exhaustion, we could barely walk. Inside the two covered trucks that were waiting we felt good to be a little protected from the piercing Baltic wind.

On our way to the factory one of the prisoners told me that the place had been bombed about a month before and was being rebuilt. We had to clear away what remained of the debris.

When we reached the plant, I understood more clearly what he had meant. Beams, stones, broken machines—all were so damaged and entangled that we hardly knew where to start. A few civilians were supervising the work. They were as hard as any SS officer, and they watched us constantly, making certain that we worked every moment without a pause.

The work was painful. The beams were metal, and because we had no gloves, our skin stuck to them. The stones were very heavy and hard to move. We had to put all the material in small wagons mounted on wheels too little to roll in the snow. One of the civilians watched two of us pushing an immovable wagon with all our strength. "You lazy good-for-nothing. I am going to show you how to work." He called another civilian, and they started pushing, but the wagon didn't move. I couldn't hold back a little smile. Just as my smile appeared, the supervisor stopped pushing and turned to me. "You think this is funny. Well, I am going to report you to your SS officer and he will erase your smile." So I was in for another special favor. I wondered what it would be this time. Ten minutes later, the supervisor returned with a soldier and pointed to me. He had meant what he said.

The work at the plant had begun at seven. When the five minute noon break finally came, we were each given one piece of bread and grease. That was all. It was too cold to sit down, and we ate our meal standing. A cup of coffee, the only warm substance we were given during the day, was served at five. At ten the work ended, though we still had the hour-long truck ride back. Considering everything, I thought that if it had not been for the cold and the metal beams that hurt my hands so badly, the work would have been easier than the railroad or the mine work. As for the soup, our only daily meal, it was barely lukewarm; but even with its bad odor and taste it was better than nothing. That night my injured shoulder was hurting; the original bandage had not been replaced and there was nothing in the building that I could use as a substitute. I tried to sleep, but again I was too cold, and I couldn't put my upcoming treatment out of my mind.

On my first Sunday back at the correction camp I rested on my board, though the cold would not let me get comfortable.

Early in the afternoon, an SS soldier and his interpreter came into the building and walked over to me. "I have a report against you stating that you insulted a supervisor.

"That is not right," I answered. "I did not say a word."

"You are not supposed to answer!" he shouted forcefully, turning on his heels. "Follow me."

They took me to the central part of the camp where they had hanged the Russian. The gallows was still there, and for a moment I was afraid they would hang me; but instead they led me to another area where there was a St. Andrew's cross, from which a victim hangs by the wrists. They fastened me to it and raised me until my feet were off the ground. The SS soldier looked at me and grinned. "Laugh all you want now. We will be back in four hours."

After about five minutes I began to feel pain in my back and shoulders. The pain became so unbearable that I fainted. I woke up when two soldiers unfastened me and let me fall to the ground. My arms felt dead, and I could not use them to get up, so the soldiers carried me to my building. Some of the other prisoners did all they could to massage my arms and warm me up. I shivered from exposure, my hands were white, and I could not move my fingers. The wound in my shoulder had reopened, and I had nothing with which to change the bandage. I stayed on my board for the rest of the day and managed to sleep a little. The following morning, the prisoners helped me get up, because I still could not move my arms. They massaged them and the movement gradually returned. It has been over fifty years since I was put on the St. Andrew's cross, but even now there are days when my arms do not function as they should.

For two weeks things were quiet, but one morning the alert sirens went off and the Germans sought shelter, leaving us exposed. I lay flat on the ground behind some big stones. The first bomb fell on the reconstructed part of the plant, and I was happy over the damage to the factory. The Germans shot at the two Russian planes and hit one. The pilot jumped out immediately and his parachute blossomed in the sky. A strong wind blew him in our direction. If he had reached the ground before the Nazis came out of hiding, we would have been able to help him; but the Germans got there when he landed and shot him to death. They weren't satisfied with having killed him, and so they booted the corpse as hard as they could. He had fallen so close to me that I could see his face. He was a young man about thirty, and the stars on his jacket indicated he was an officer.

The Russian planes had done a thorough job. They had destroyed every inch of the reconstructed part of the plant. The infuriated Nazis made us work as fast as possible to clean up, jeering at us all the while and calling us Communists. When we returned to our building that night, there were no lights on in the whole camp, and in our building the windows had been covered with black paper. There was a note warning us that anyone removing the black paper from the windows would be shot.

That night was very cold. Thick ice formed on the walls of our building. My hands had become infected, as they had been when I worked on the railroad. Suddenly I heard the door open and then close. I spoke to the man who was sleeping below me, but he did not answer. I got up as quietly as possible and made my way to the door. Before I reached the door, a voice said, "Ruski, Ruski." I lit a match and saw an emaciated Russian in his officer's uniform. He made a gesture to shake hands with me. I turned toward the rest of the prisoners. "There is a Russian prisoner here."

One of the men lit a piece of candle, and then I saw the Russian more clearly. He was about twenty-five years old and very thin. None of us spoke Russian, but he knew French well enough to converse. He said that he had brought a few cigarettes that he wanted to trade for bread. The Nazis were leaving the Russians to starve to death. They were afraid of the Russians and never made them work, and since they did not work, they did not eat. Once in a while, a soldier would take them a bucket of soup, but that soldier was accompanied by five others with machine guns. He told us that every day some of his friends died from sickness or starvation. We did not take his cigarettes, but we gave him what was left of our soup—all we had to offer. He was so famished that he swallowed it as if it were a drop of water. When he said he was leaving, we cautioned him about the dogs, but he smiled and opened his jacket. He had a bayonet. He didn't say how he had managed to get it and keep it from the Nazis.

Just then we heard footsteps by the door, and we hid him under a bed. It was the sergeant. "What is going on here?" he bellowed. "One of the men is sick. We are taking care of him." The sergeant came in, "Where is he?" he asked. "Right here." One prisoner sat by the side of his bed and held his side. "What is the matter with you?" asked the sergeant. "I have a bellyache."

The order was given for all of us to be counted. They would probably find the Russian, kill him, and then punish us very severely. After they counted us several times, the sergeant told us to return to our beds. They had not found him. We waited awhile and when everything seemed to be quiet, we told the Russian that he could go. He did not appear to be afraid, and it seemed that he would have enjoyed staying with us. What happened to him I do not know, for I never saw him again.

I had ten days left on my sentence, and the short time gave me a little courage to keep going. It was Sunday, and every other Sunday we had showers. At other times the only water we had to wash with was our drinking water. Before noon that morning, the guards took us to the showers. It was a cold day, and the snow was iced over.

On the way we passed the Russians. Their uniforms were much worse than ours, though we wore rags. When they saw us, they began to motion with friendly gestures. The guards began to hit us with their rifles while the men in the watchtower fired at the five Russians. One of them opened what was left of his shirt and made gestures to indicate that only cowards shot unarmed people. Then he indicated his hatred for the Germans by spitting at them. A soldier shot him, and the other Russians ran to assist him, but the Germans kept shooting at their feet to keep them from getting near him.

When we reached the showers, which were in the open, there was neither soap nor towels. A soldier guarded us with a machine gun as we undressed. When I turned on the water, it came out icy cold but quickly changed to hot. We protested that the water was not right, but the soldier only laughed. I was freezing, and though I had not been able to shower, I was nonetheless wet. The temperature was below zero, and I shook uncontrollably as I hurriedly put on my clothes. One prisoner explained to me that the showers were usually pleasant, but on that day the Nazis were punishing us for sympathizing with the Russians.

In the afternoon the SS commandant came to see us. The same French interpreter was with him.

> On your feet! I heard of the demonstration that took place on the way to the showers. If you are friends of the Russians, you must be Communists, too, so you are enemies of the Reich. Consequently, you will stay here fifteen days longer than you were supposed to. If there is another demonstration like today's, you will stay here an extra three months. Tonight you will not eat, and tomorrow you will do forty-five minutes of exercise before going to work. Those of you who will

feel tired will be given a special opportunity to rest in the fresh air.

We all knew what he meant—the iron boxes. They were about ten feet long, five feet wide, and five feet high. A man could lie down or sit but he could not stand. Confinement could last from a few hours to several days, with no food or water. Many prisoners had died in those cages. Whereas the cold was intolerable in winter, during the summer months the metal became so hot that the prisoners would slowly suffocate.

The following morning, the French interpreter came to tell us that we would start the exercise at eight. When the men began to curse him, he became angry. "I shall inform the commandant of your attitude, and you will do a full hour of exercise. If you like, we can add another half hour." Ten minutes later the commandant came, and we started the exercise. The first thing I knew, I was hit on the shoulder, and the directions came at us rapidly: run, stop, sit, stand, flat on the ground. The guards ran with us but, because they were replaced every few minutes, never had a chance to become tired. After ten minutes I reacted more slowly, and the guards were hitting me on the head to make me move faster. Finally, I fainted. The cold snow against my face brought me back to consciousness.

An SS officer stood before me. "I see your health is not good. I have decided to give you a day to rest. That will help you feel better." Two soldiers dragged me by the feet to the cooler. One walked into it, pulling me by the arms, while the other held my feet. I wanted to kick him in the face, but I was too exhausted. They closed the door and locked it from the outside.

I had been trembling and sweating when they put me

in, but I immediately began to freeze. I sat with my back against the iron wall. I was afraid to go to sleep and freeze to death, or wake up with my hands or feet frozen. My legs became rigid up to my knees, and moving my fingers grew difficult. I decided to rub myself as long as I had the strength, because I could not feel my feet any more and my ears were burning. I gathered myself in a huddle, to make use of my body heat, and I fought off panic. Suppose the SS forgot about me. I imagined spending sixteen hours instead of the eight he intended, thinking I could not survive.

As the hours passed I became more or less unconscious until I heard dogs growling. It sounded like three of them, throwing themselves against the door. I was not afraid of them, as the door was very solid, so I began to tease them, hoping that their noise would get someone's attention, but nothing happened. There was only a little crack at the hinges, and I could not tell whether it was daylight, but I knew that the dogs moved freely around the camp at night.

What seemed like a short time later I was hardly conscious when the door opened and a soldier came in to see if I was dead. When he saw that I was still alive, he told me to get up and walk out. He could have told me a thousand times, but I could not move. He called for another soldier, and the two of them took me out into the brightness of daylight. When I closed my eyes and fell on the snow, they picked me up by the arms and tried to steady me, but my legs simply refused to support me. One soldier said, "Try to move your legs. We'll take you to your building and give you some hot coffee. Then you'll feel better." I tried to move my legs and eventually took a few steps. The cooler was only a few minutes from the building, but I felt as if it were miles away.

Instead of going straight to my building, the guards took me to a canteen on our way. Inside, several soldiers were eating and drinking. When they saw me, they began to speak in lowered voices. Perhaps it was the first time that a prisoner had been permitted inside the canteen. One of my guards went to speak with the others and then returned. "I am going to give you coffee and bread. Please do not tell anyone what we're doing for you. If the SS found out, we would be reprimanded and you would go back to the cooler." I promised not to say anything and thanked him the best I could, while my hands shook so that I could hardly hold the cup. However, it was the best cup of coffee I ever had in my life, and the food helped restore me. The same guard said, "We'll take you back to your building in about a half hour. We picked you up one hour early." After a few more cups of coffee, my hands began to feel warm, and I got up without help when it was time to go.

The SS officer was waiting for me when I reached the building. He was so fat that he looked all puffed up. "I hope that you feel much better after eight hours of complete rest." I did not answer but looked at him with all the hatred that I felt. "Do not look at me like that or I'll send you back to the cooler. Tomorrow, you will go back to work. Your assignment is to bury some Russian prisoners. They are so unhealthy that they die like flies, and their corpses cause disease." Before leaving, he added, "I want you to do your work; I do not want any epidemic of disease in this building, you understand." I nodded.

I was happy to have the rest of the day to recuperate. My feet and legs were still cold, but I had stopped shaking. That night when the men returned from work, I learned that eight men, including myself, had been confined to the coolers, and two were still there. Later on, when the soup came, I ate all I could. It was warmer than usual, and bad though it was, it made me feel better.

The Russian camp was encircled with barbed wire. A guard opened the gate, and as we filed in, we each received a pickax or shovel. We started digging at the very place that the Russian had been shot three days earlier, and by seven that night, though we were not finished, it was time to return to our building. We had not seen a single Russian all day long.

The next day we resumed work. I was puzzled by the size of the pit we were digging. How many Russians had died? During the day we saw perhaps ten of them, and our guards were very nervous. Something was going on, but the Russians never said a word. They stared at the hole we were digging with fear in their faces. We finished the pit that night, and before we left, the SS officer asked the guards whether any of us needed to be punished. One of them answered that we were all working hard. The officer looked at us and with a hard voice said, "I see that the cooler was good for some of you. The next time you need it, the punishment will last twice as long."

It was the first time I could really look at the fat officer. He was ugly and walked with his legs apart. As soon as he turned around, a Russian threw a knife at him. It was aimed at his heart but hit him in the shoulder. One of the guards shot the Russian, while others forced all his companions back into their building. The SS officer was bleeding badly. The whole blade was inside the shoulder; we could see only the handle. Two Soldiers helped him reach his car.

We were stupefied to think a prisoner had tried to kill the SS officer, since there was nothing to gain. If he died, the next one might be worse. Yet I could understand. The Russians were starving to death, and since they would die one way or another, they weren't concerned about their lives. They were men of courage, more fearless than the Nazis.

With our guards, we went into the cells to pick up the dead. In the first cell, the Russians regarded us with apparent hostility, but one of them explained that they knew what we were doing. Their situation was awful. They had to sleep on the cement floor, and they were indeed being starved to death. Many were emaciated, and the legs of some who were near death were covered with wounds full of pus. There were no dead in that first cell. In the next cell the silent hostility was the same, but again it was not us whom they blamed. We picked up two puffy bodies of men who had been dead for days. Carrying them by the arms and feet, we took them outside and put them into large bags. By four that afternoon we had cleared the cells of some twenty bodies.

A truck drove the bodies to the pit we had dug and unloaded its cargo as if it were dumping a load of stones. We were forced to go into the pit and line up the bodies, and it remains the most horrible experience I have had in my life. Some of their eyes were opened and seemed to be looking at us reproachfully. In some cases, the skin had ruptured, leaking a putrid liquid as we walked over the bodies. I got out of the pit sick to my stomach and nearly out of my mind.

The following morning it was already bright daylight by the time the soldiers came for us. As soon as we were in formation, we started marching toward the center of the camp. Everything was quiet, but I sensed that something was wrong. When we reached the center, an SS officer in black uniform climbed a few steps of the gallows and spoke to us through the loudspeaker system. "A Russian has seriously injured the commandant of this camp and has paid for the crime with his life. We are taking steps to make certain that such a criminal act will not be repeated. We have decided to shoot fifty Russians, and since you are their friends and therefore Communists as they are, it is only natural that you should participate. Fifty of you, one per cell block, will be selected to choose the Russians who will be shot. Anyone who refuses will stay here three more months." As the message was translated into French, Polish, English, and Serbian, I worried about being chosen, for I knew that I would never be able to do it. I would accept my fate and spend three months at the camp. We had the rest of the day off and were served soup even though we had not worked.

In the morning after the counts, we returned to our building. The section leader chose a man, wrote down his prison number, and left without a word. The man began to shake. "I will not do it. I'll stay here three more months, but I won't be responsible for murder."

The next morning we got up at daybreak and a half hour later were in the Russian camp. Standing outside were about three hundred prisoners, only a fraction of the entire body. I could not understand the reason behind their selection. Soldiers armed with machine guns surrounded the fifty men who were to choose. The soldiers urged the men forward, but when not one prisoner moved, they began hitting the men with their guns. Most of them fell. The leader shouted at the top of his voice, "After the execution, I will take special care of you for not obeying my orders."

The commandant then chose fifty Russians at random. They knew what was in store for them, and they started singing as they were lined up. Ten soldiers faced them at a distance of about fifty feet. The clatter of machine guns broke into the singing, and a few seconds later it was quiet.

No one moved until the SS officer ordered my group to put the dead in the pit. Why he chose us I never found out; perhaps it was because of the demonstration on the way to the showers. We dragged the dead by their feet. As I was handling one of them, he moved. There was nothing I could do but set him down on the pile as gently as I could. The pit had looked very large when we dug it; but the bodies were now well above the ground, even though we had lined them up to save all possible space.

A truck driven by a German civilian backed up to the mass grave and the driver dumped a load of quicklime, covering all the bodies. Just then I heard a cry coming from the pit and I trembled with horror. The soldier answered by firing several volleys into the grave. The commandant, who had watched all impassively, slapped his gloves against his leg and walked away.

The next day was Saturday, and we went to work as usual. Shortly after we returned for the night, the camp director came in. He had lost several pounds and his left arm was in a sling. He seemed upset as he spoke to us. "Prisoners, most of you are due to leave soon when your work for the Reich comes to an end. During these last few days I do not want to hear of any incident of any kind; otherwise, you will all be treated the same." Then he came over to me. "You have only four days left, but I can always change my mind and keep you longer."

At the factory we began to clear away debris that had been created by the Russian plane. From the aggressive attitude of the civilian supervisors we suspected that the news from the Russian front was not good at all. We had only one fifteen minute break during the whole day.

They pushed us as fast as possible, because they couldn't resume reconstruction until we had cleared everything away. Tuesday was my last day, and I worked diligently, not wanting anything to keep me from leaving on Wednesday.

That morning one of the civilians called to me, but there were four of us working together, and so I paid no attention to him, even though I was fairly certain that he was calling me. He was becoming impatient, and he came closer and pointed at me. "You pig, can't you answer when I call you? Follow me. I have a special job for you." I controlled my temper and followed him.

He took me to another corner of the plant and pointed

into an excavation some ten feet deep. "My measuring tape has fallen into the debris. Go and get it." The excavation contained many large stones piled head high. From the way he looked at me, I suspected that he wanted me to refuse, but I was not about to expose myself to three more months of camp life. Cautiously I went down and picked up the tape. I crawled back up as carefully as possible, hoping that I wouldn't dislodge a stone and start all of them falling. When I reached the top, I threw the tape at him. "Pick it up and give it to me," he said.

Wednesday was the day of my departure. I went to work as usual but no one spoke to me and nothing happened. I became worried, but at noon two soldiers came to pick me up in a truck. With about fifteen other prisoners I was taken back to my building, where the commandant was waiting for us with another of his speeches. "You will be leaving this camp in one hour. I am speaking to you because I take a great interest in you. It would be much better that you never return here. If you do, I will be forced to take special disciplinary measures to educate you as you will deserve. A truck will take you to the station." He was still quite pale, but his arm was out of the sling. I was glad never to have to look at him again.

A cattle car awaited us at the railroad station. Only fifteen were loaded into the car, and since it was not cold, the ride would be pleasant. I stretched out on the floor to relax, and the train started moving. I wondered whether we were going east or west. At our stopover that night I tried unsuccessfully to see where we were, but I could not even hear the guards on duty around the car. They kept us locked inside, and since there were no latrines in the car, we decided to use one end of the car for that purpose.

Early in the morning, when the train started rolling again, I tried looking through a crack to see the name of the station, but I saw no sign. By the afternoon I was convinced that we were returning west, probably to the old camp run by Ernst Vogel. After two days in the cattle car, we were hungry and thirsty and anxious for fresh air. That night, when the train stopped, a soldier opened the door, and the smell from inside the car backed him up. Pointing at one of the men he told him to clean up the mess. The man asked, "With what?" The answer was, "With your hands."

We were lined up by the station while the prisoner finished his cleaning job. When he joined us, the soldier came back, holding a bag in his hands. "See how well I take care of you. I brought each of you a bologna sandwich." It was our first food in two days. The man who had cleaned the car had not been given a chance to wash his hands. He said he was not hungry, but the soldier insisted, "You are hungry as well as the others, and you are going to eat, or I'm sending you right back to the camp."

The man took the sandwich and ate up to where his fingers held the bread. The soldier smirked at him. "Eat every bit of it I don't want a crumb left over." The prisoner finished it, but he quickly vomited. "Pig!" cried the soldier. "You deserve to be made to eat what you threw up." He did not insist, however.

We traveled until we reached the old camp. It was almost empty, and there were about twenty men I did not know, one of whom occupied my old bed. My former companions had been moved to some other place. About six the next morning, Vogel came to welcome us. "I have come to meet the new prisoners. There is one among you whom I have known for a long time," he said, looking directly at me. "I hope your stay at the correction camp has inspired you to continue to work for the Reich. I want to inform you that I will not fool with you one more time. If I receive one report against you, I will turn you over to the Gestapo. I am sending you to work on a farm where there is only an older couple." I didn't like his smile when he said it, but I was quiet.

The small farm where I was sent to work was a couple of miles from the camp. When I arrived at the house, a man of about sixty opened the door and let me in. "Come in. Do not be afraid," he said softly. I had heard that before, and I was cautious. "Sit down," he continued. "My wife is preparing your breakfast. First you must eat, then we can talk about the work." In a moment she had the table ready for me. She looked me over.

"You are skinny. You need to eat well. If you are still hungry when you are finished, tell me and I'll bring you some more. We are going to take good care of you. You will be well treated here with us."

The man explained the reasons for their kindness. During the First World War he had been a prisoner of the French and for three years had worked on a farm. The farmers had been kind to him, and he never forgot it. Now he wanted to do the same for me. Although it was against the law, he wanted me to eat with them at the table. However, he said, he would prepare a little table in the side room by the kitchen, in case someone should happen to drop in during a meal. Then I would need only to move quickly to the little table. He added, "If what you are wearing is all that you have, you need something else. We'll find something for you and do your washing once a week."

I could not believe it. When I told the man that I had just returned from a correction camp in Poland, he held his head with both hands. "I know the SS methods. I am German but not Nazi. Our two sons are, though, and when they come here, I have to act as though I were a party member. I expect them next month during their furlough. You will have to eat on your little table, but everything will go well." I was reminded of Gras Double's two sons. There was nothing for me to do but wait and see. The man spoke again. "When you have finished your breakfast, I'll show you the farm and then you may rest in the barn until noon. I'll call you when the meal is ready."

It was a small farm with no more than fifteen animals. As we walked the field, he struck me as an honest man whom I could trust. I slept until noon, when he woke me for the meal. Afterward he let me rest all day until five, when it was time to attend to the animals. By six I was finished and went to the house to eat. During the evening meal they both spoke to me as if I were their house guest. I returned to the camp after dinner, feeling fine. After three years of struggle, I thanked God for the newfound blessing and prayed that it would continue.

The next day, I asked the man why he kept a prisoner with so little work to do. He told me that he was aging and that even though the farm was small and didn't really support them, he liked to have someone to take care of the outside work so that he could devote more time to his repair shop. He felt that he was ahead that way and could make ends meet, but also he was glad to take one man away from the Nazis and provide him with a more peaceful existence while he was a war prisoner. "You must know that Germany is falling fast," he said in a lowered tone. "It may not be long before you can return to your own country."

I was amazed at the man's words and at the couple's kindness. The food was delicious and there was plenty. The work was easy, I was my own boss, and I could rest when I wanted to. My health improved tremendously, and I was as happy as any war prisoner could be. I had even forgotten about his two sons. One morning while I was currying the horses, I jumped with surprise at a loud "Heil Hitler." Two Nazis were behind me.

"What are you doing here?" asked one of them.

"Currying the horses, as you can see."

"Where are our parents? They are not in the house."

"I have no idea. It is possible that they went out."

"Be careful when you speak to officers of the Third Reich," said the other, who was wearing the iron cross.

They exchanged a few words in lowered voices and then spoke loudly enough for me to hear. "The house was not locked. How can our parents leave the house with a prisoner around? He is probably waiting for his chance to take everything they have and then set the house on fire."

I began to lose my patience. "I may be a prisoner of war, but I am not a criminal. I have no intention of setting anything on fire or robbing anyone. Since I have been in your country, I have known more criminals than there are in France."

"Don't be insolent or we will have you arrested by the Gestapo."

They left, insulting me. I would have been wiser not to say a word. Once more I had spoken too much, and I might be in trouble again. A few minutes later the old couple came back. The sons greeted their parents with "Heil Hitler," which the father answered simply by raising his right arm. They seemed to ignore their mother, and they began to talk about me, pointing to the barn. I wanted to speak to the old man as soon as possible and find out if he could protect me. He immediately came to find out what had happened. "Why did you speak to Willy and Karl?

Had I not told you that they were Nazis? This could have very serious consequences for you. I will try to excuse you the best I can, hoping that they will forget the incident, but do not do that again."

At noon I ate at the little table and listened as Willy and Karl narrated the German victory along the Russian front. The father listened but never responded. He knew their statements were false. The wife asked me if I needed a second serving. Suddenly Karl was behind her. "I forbid you to give him a second serving. One is enough. After all, we are at war and he is a prisoner." He glared at me as he towered above me and my small table. "My parents are too good to you. For the time being I am the boss, and I intend to teach you how to work and obey. Now that you have finished eating, return to work instantly."

I left quickly so as not to cause problems for the father. I still had fifteen minutes left of my noon break, so I went to the barn and stretched out in the hay. I had been there a few minutes when I heard someone coming. It was Karl again. He had changed his uniform for civilian clothes and was ready for work. "What are you doing there? Do you intend to sleep all day? Truly, the French are the laziest people in the world. Get up. Prepare the horses. We are going to spread the manure over my father's field."

We worked all afternoon without talking to each other. I was worried, and I decided to beg Karl's forgiveness as soon as we returned to the farm. We went back about five. The father was in the yard with Willy. I had to take the chance. I told Willy and Karl that I was very sorry for having spoken to them, and I begged them to forgive me. I explained that I did not realize what I had said to them;

otherwise, I would not have spoken that way. Having been away from home for three years, I was not always rational.

When I finished, Karl said, "Very well, we accept your apology. If you had not begged for our forgiveness, we would have reported you tonight to the mayor, though our father did not want us to. But we won't report you, and we'll forget the incident because our father needs you. But, believe me, we are doing that for him and not for you. Just one final word of warning. Watch your words and be ready to obey at all times. That is your only right." Again I had narrowly escaped.

The next morning, the father came to the barn looking worried. He explained that early in the year he had killed a pig and that now he needed to kill another one, though it was strictly forbidden by the Nazis to kill more than one animal a year. He had explained to his sons that he and their mother were not well and needed extra food. He believed that the sons had understood and would not denounce him for committing such an infraction.

"Are you willing to help me kill the pig? You must understand that if we are caught, it will be considered a crime. I would prefer to do it after my sons left, but I need their help, too. It will take all five of us to do the job quickly, without attracting anyone's attention. Understand that you do not have to take any part in it. I am not ordering you; I am only asking you." I quickly answered, "You can depend on me. I'll help you." He cautioned me again. "If we are caught, the penalty is five years in jail."

For me that would mean imprisonment until death by torture, but the old man and his wife were so kind to me that I felt an obligation to take the risk. "I'll help you," I assured him. "Very well," he said. "We'll kill the pig tomorrow morning."

I knew the old man returned my trust. For example, he had revealed to me a supply of butter hidden under the kitchen floor. It was forbidden by Nazi law for the farmers to make any butter, since everything had to go to the German army. The police could make a search at any time if they had an inkling that the law had been broken.

The next morning, when I reached the farm, everything was ready. Without saying a word, we all worked as hard and as fast as we could. The man filled the pig's mouth with some dough to reduce the noise, and one of the sons killed it. Everything went fine. By noon, all was pretty much under control, and we went to the house to eat. The sons were very nervous. We were eating when someone knocked on the door. I was at my little table, but I could hear and see everything. The sons became pale, but the father very calmly called to the person at the door. "Come right in. The door is open."

It was a sergeant accompanied by two MP's. "Heil Hitler," the sergeant said in a formal manner. "I have a warrant signed by the mayor to search your house. It seems that you are stocking food against the law." The sons looked stricken. Then Karl bolted from his chair. "This is ridiculous. How can you accuse our parents that way? My brother and I just returned from the Russian front. We are Nazis and are devoted to the party. If any such thing was going on in this house, we would denounce our father. We could not tolerate his keeping for himself what belongs to the German army." The reply calmed the sergeant, but he persisted. "I understand, but I must do my job."

They conducted a superficial search and found nothing. "What do you have in the barn?" the sergeant asked. The old man answered. "A few pigs, two cows, a few sheep, and two horses. Would you like to see them? You may go if you wish." The sergeant replied, "No, that will not be necessary. I trust you." He left with the two soldiers.

Although we had been very careful with the pig, someone had apparently denounced the old man. He was impatient. "Let's return to the barn and destroy all traces of evidence. The mayor will not be satisfied with this search. He will order a complete search of the house and the barn. We have no time to lose. They may return at any moment." Willy panicked. He got up and started shouting at Karl. "I did not want to have a part in this, but you forced me. I am going to denounce you. I will explain that I was ignorant of everything, that I belong to the party, and that I wear the iron cross. They will believe me."

The father ran to his bedroom and returned in a moment, pointing a gun at Willy. "If you move, I'll shoot you before you have time to leave this room. You and your Hitler and your Nazi party. After you leave, if you denounce us, your mother and I will kill ourselves rather than fall into the hands of the Gestapo. Now, everyone to the barn."

The sons walked before the old man, and the mother cried silently. I followed them to the barn, and the farmer told me to leave the door slightly open and to watch while they attended to the pig. If I saw anyone, I was to go meet them and say that everyone had gone to the neighbors and would be back soon.

That would give us time to cover the remaining evidence with hay. They would then leave by the door that opened to the road and would return to the house without being seen.

I was afraid to think what would happen to me if Willy denounced his father. I was certain that the couple would shoot themselves rather than be arrested by the Gestapo. How could I have become mixed up in such a situation?

The family worked quickly and silently. The pig was not very big, but it would provide food for several months. The farmer said that at midnight he would take part of it to store at the home of a friend. Then all would be safe. By seven everything was clean, and no one had come back to search. As I was leaving to walk back to the camp, the farmer's wife apologized for not having had time to serve a meal, and she offered me a sandwich. I put it in my pocket and left.

The following morning when I arrived at the farm, the old man met me at the door. "You're free to ask to be sent to another place. I don't want you to take further risks because of me. You aren't guilty of anything." I knew that I couldn't leave easily or without guilt feelings about both of them.

"You're so kind to me, and I'm so well off here that I'll take my chances and stay." We went inside and I walked to my little table. Willy and Karl greeted me with "Heil Hitler," but I didn't respond.

After breakfast I went to the barn and started to work.

There was no visible evidence of the slaughter. The farmer had evidently taken the meat to his friend's home. The day passed with no sign of a search party, and I began to breathe more easily.

A few days later, just as I arrived for work, the two sons, dressed in uniform, were preparing to leave. After an unemotional conversation they left. The farmer didn't return their "Heil Hitler," and his wife was crying.

Time passed quietly. I did the best I could to take care of the farm. Soon it was December, 1943, with Christmas just around the corner. One day we sat and talked about the war. "I believe this is going to be your last Christmas away from home," the old man said. I remained skeptical. "I don't share your confidence. I now believe that Germany will fall, but the army must still be very strong. With only the Russian front to maintain, the Nazis can run the show for quite a while. Of course, with the Americans in the picture, things will change." That night, I thought about our conversation. Was it possible that he could be right? Or was he only making idle chat?

The cold, rainy weather had returned. The farmer did not want to leave me outside unless it was necessary, and so I assisted him in his repair shop. One day I was working in the barn when a sergeant came. "Are you the prisoner with the number 38952?" I began to shake, but I had to answer. I said in a low voice, "Yes."

"Pick up your things. You are coming with me."

"Where to?"

"France. You are going home."

It could not be true. The sergeant saw that I did not believe him, and he handed me a paper covered with several legal stamps. The document stated my name, prisoner's number, and pardon. The reason given for the pardon was that my father, being old, would need me to take care of his farm. My old lie! I could not believe my eyes. I was about to follow the soldier when the farmer appeared. "What do you want with my prisoner?" he insisted gruffly. "I brought his papers," the sergeant answered. "He is being sent back to France."

At first the old man was stunned, and then he smiled and grabbed me by the shoulders. "Do you remember what I told you? I was right. Before you go, come to the house to pay your respects to my wife. She will prepare a lunch for you." He took the sergeant by the arm. "Come in and have coffee with us." A few minutes later I was ready to leave. The wife cried and the man shook my hand, holding it a long time. They had been like a family to me, and I could not thank them enough.

When the men returned to camp that night, I explained that I had been freed, but they didn't react as I expected– they already knew about it. I was to leave the next morning, and I hardly slept that night.

The following morning I was on a train going west. I sat between two ladies who stared at me and moved themselves as far away from me as they could, as though I were a skunk. We rode for ten hours until we reached Stargard, the central camp in Pomerania. A soldier checked my papers and accompanied me to camp Stalag IID, where a blackout was in effect. Inside my block there were many other prisoners, and no one paid any particular attention to me.

I went to bed and promptly fell asleep. The next morning I noticed that all the prisoners were resting; no one was moving about. I asked one man if I was in the right place to be sent back to France. "You're in the right place, man," he said listlessly. "I've already spent two months here. Every day I hope to leave, but I'm still here. Some of the men have been waiting for more than three months. "

All the men looked lifeless, and I soon understood why. They were not working; therefore, they received no food other than a single cup of soup every day at one, barely enough to keep them alive. The daily meal was distributed outside. We had to form a line and wait to be served. Many of the men could barely drag themselves up, and they had to be helped because of their weakened condition. I returned to my bed to eat my soup, a thick white paste that didn't smell too bad. The old couple had spoiled me, so that now I had to readjust myself to bad food.

The camp consisted of about twenty cellblocks. We were free to walk around and visit as we pleased, since the count was done only once a day. As I became acquainted with some of the prisoners, we discussed our situation. The men were disheartened with waiting. All we could do was lie in bed most of the time. Day by day I grew weaker as the bad diet began to get the best of me. When I had to stand up, I felt dizzy. We had no showers, but there was some water next to the latrines where we could wash ourselves off. Within a month I felt as bad as the others. I lived only for the daily cup of soup. I was too weak to do anything else.

The only thing that broke the boredom of waiting was my discovery that I had become infested with ticks. A month passed, and I gave up the possibility of returning to France. It grew cold. We had been given only two blankets, but they helped very little, since there was no heat in the building. We stayed in bed all of the time.

I was there two and a half months when rumors began to circulate that a train was being hooked up for us.

The rumors gave us courage and lifted our morale, but our spirits sank again after a week had passed and nothing happened. At the end of another month an officer came quite suddenly one day to tell us to pick up our things. There was an explosion of joy. Some of the men were in a dying condition by then, but we helped one another into the trucks.

A passenger train was reserved for us, with eight seats in each compartment; there was no hall to connect the compartments to each other. At first it seemed nice, but once the train started moving, it continued for hours without a stop. There were no latrines, and we were virtually caged in the train for two days and two nights, barely able to move, and sick, hungry, and thirsty. I felt stiff all over and could no longer move my legs.

On the third morning, when the train stopped at a station, I saw many members of the German Red Cross. An officer speaking through a megaphone told us that there would be a brief rest stop for us. Almost every one of us had to be helped by the nurses to reach the converted rest room. When we returned to our compartment, we were given bread, margarine, and sausage, and as much drinking water as we wanted. The train began to move again after two hours. It took six days to reach the French border.

We had heard stories that some trains with French prisoners had gone as far as the French border and then returned to Germany, and that many of the prisoners had killed themselves rather than return to Germany. Only one mile away from the French border our train stopped for many hours. Then suddenly it moved again and we crossed the border. During that night we could see nothing in the blackout, but we knew that we were in France.

The station was full of people waiting for us when we reached Compiegne the following afternoon. The French orderlies took care of those who were too sick to walk, while others like myself were helped to a barracks about a mile away. Right away we had a good shower in a heated room with soap and a towel. Next, we were placed in a dorm where each bed had a real mattress. There was plenty of food, and we could eat all we wanted. A French orderly told me that all this had been ordered for us by the German authorities. Well attended and very well fed, I began to put on some weight. At the end of two weeks we were given new uniforms and informed that we would be taken to Paris the following day.

We were to take a first-class train, dressed in our new clothes. The German officers themselves helped us to the train station. Some German newsmen asked to take pictures and offered cigars, which we all refused. The sergeant was most displeased with our refusal, but because of the camera he had to smile. A press agent with a movie camera gave his thanks to the Germans and left. As soon as he was out of sight, one of the German officers raged at us. "You pigs have no appreciation for any kindness. We have freed you, we have been taking care of you for weeks, and we are offering you a friendly hand; but pigs like you do not know how to appreciate the good things. You had better be very careful. We are the masters here and we could send you back to Germany." Having said his little piece, he left, and we walked into the first-class cars for the ride.

That day was March 6, 1944. All during the trip, I looked out the window, entranced by the scenery of my homeland. It was the end of my life as a prisoner of war. I had spent 1,379 days as a prisoner.

Our train reached Paris by the northern station.

Epilogue

After his release by the Germans in a prisoner exchange, Claude Letulle fought in the French underground until the end of the war. He did not marry the fiancee he had left in Paris. After the war, he moved to the United States and lived in Boston for two years. He then moved to Louisiana where he lives today. Letulle wrote this memoir at the request of his wife, to help ease the pain of his recurring nightmares.

The author in 1947

Official Documents

Note:

Some of the documents list May 25, 1940, as the date of the author's capture. May 25 is actually the day he was listed as officially missing in action. His capture occurred on June 22, after four weeks of trying to avoid the Nazi invaders. Likewise, February 3, 1943 is listed as the official date of the author's release. However, the German government withheld his release papers until December of that year and it was not until early in 1944 that he actually arrived back in France as a free man.

Card #3874 issued to Claude Letulle by the United States Holocaust Memorial Museum, where a copy of *Nightmare Memoir* has been made part of the permanent book collection.

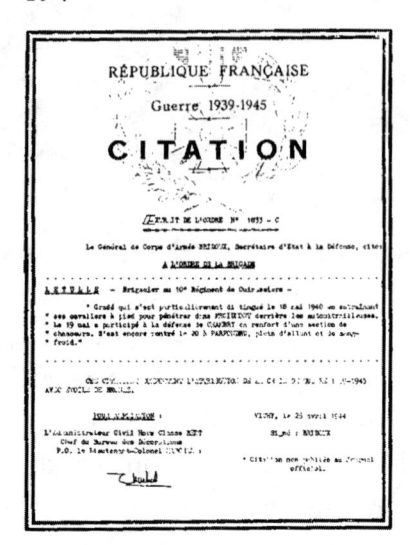

Croix de Guerre citation issued to the author in 1944

Translation:

French Republic

War 1939-1945

CITATION

Extract of Order No. 1833-C

General of the Army Corps Bridoux, Secretary of State for Defense, states:

By Order of the Brigade

LETULLE — Corporal in the 10th Regiment of Cuirassiers —

"A noncommissioned officer who particularly distinguished himself on May 18, 1940, while leading his troop to penetrate Froidmont behind the light armored cars. On May 19 he participated in the defense of Chambry as reinforcement for a platoon of infantry. Moreover, on May 20 he appeared at Parfondru, full of initiative and composure."

These citations involve the awarding of the Croix de Guerre 1939-1945 with a bronze star.

True Copy: Unclassified Civil Administrator Bert/Head of the Bureau of Decorations/By order of Lieutenant-Colonel Marchal

Nightmare Memoir

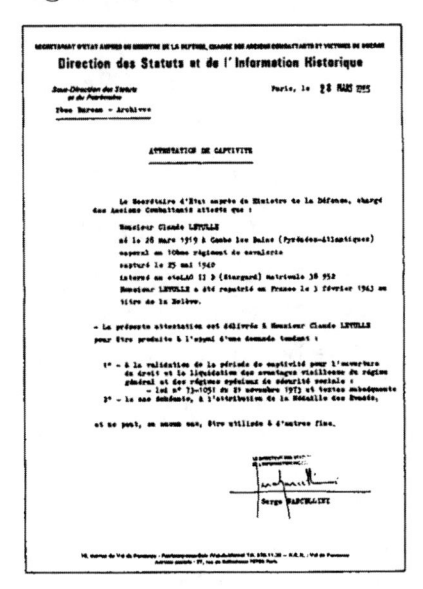

Proof of captivity issued to the author by the Secretary of State, Department of Veterans and Victims of War

Translation:

Secretary of State for the Minister of Defense, Department of Veterans and Victims of War

Administration of Laws and Historical Information

PROOF OF CAPTIVITY

The Secretary of State for the Minister of Defense, Department of Veterans, attests that:

Mister Claude Letulle / born March 28, 1919, at Combo-les-Bains (Département of Pyrennées-Atlantiques) / corporal in the 10th Regiment of Cavalry/ was captured May 25, 1940 / interned at Stalag II-D (Stargard), prisoner number 38-952 / Mr. Letulle was retruned to France on February 3, 1943, through troop rotation.

This document is delivered to Mr. Claude Letulle to be used in response to any questions pertaining to: / 1. The validation of the term of his captivity for use in legal matters and for access to old-age benefits and special social security benefits (Law Number 73-1051 of November 21, 1973) / 2. If necessary for obtaining the award of the Medal of Escapees. / And it cannot in any case be used for other purposes.

The Author's Medals

In addition to the Croix de Guerre, Claude Letulle received other decorations for his bravery as a soldier, prisoner, and resistance fighter. A description of some of these awards appeared in The Journal of the Orders and Medals Society of America, *The Medal Collector,* in the July 1990 issue. Major Fred Borch, III, writing for the Journal, recounted some of the background for the awards:

> Letulle was drafted shortly after France declared war on Germany in September, 1939. He received basic training in the Seine-Marne area, and arrived on the front three months later. On May 9, 1940, Letulle and his tank unit, the 10th Regiment of Cuirassiers, arrived in Sedan, on the border between France and Germany. The next day, the German Wehrmacht and Waffen-SS broke through the French defenses, and the Frnch Army began a retreat.
>
> Separated from his own unit after a few days, Letulle and a few companions joined up with other French forces and fought the Germans as best they could. But the French continued to be beaten, and retreated further.
>
> On May 18, 1940, Corporal Letulle fought in the defense of Chambry in support of an infantry unit. On May 19, 1940, he and his comrades arrived in the little town of Parfondru and joined a regiment of French infantry. Its commander heard a SOS on the radio- a group of 250 French soldiers were almost surrounded by the Germans and were pinned down by intense fire. They were in great need of ammunition, and Letulle's commander asked for volunteers to take ammunition to them. Letulle was the only volunteer.
>
> For this act of bravery on May 19, 1940, Letulle received the Medaille Militaire (1939-1945).

This medal, created in 1852, is roughly equivalent to the British Distinguished Conduct Medal. It is awarded only to generals and admirals in command, and to noncommissioned officers who especially distiguish themselves in combat.

The Medaille Militaire takes precedence over the Croix de Guerre, being a superior gallantry award.

Letulle also was decorated with the French Croix de Guerre with Bronze Star by the General of the Army Corps. According to the official citation, Letulle's gallantry between May 18-20 was the basis for the award.

Letulle says, however, that his Croix De Guerre with Bronze Star was awarded for his rescue of one of his company sergeants. On May 19, 1940, Letulle risked his own life to carry this wounded man under heavy fire to a Red Cross truck. Letulle's belief that he was rewarded for this gallant rescue shows that in combat nothing is more important to a soldier than the life of a fellow soldier, and that a superior may reward an act of bravery far different from that prized by the soldier.

According to Major Borch, Claude Letulle reported that he received the Medaille de Prisonniers with a lapel pin in the form of a piece of barbed wire. However, Letulle is entitled to wear the War Commemorative Medal with two clasps: France (for his services in the war) and Liberation (for his resistance activities). He is also entitled to wear a "Bar for the Wounded" on this medal.

Joining the Resistance upon his release was a particular act of bravery. Not only because he had been through so much as a prisoner, but also because the punishment meted out to former POWs who were caught resisting the Third Reich was immediate execution.

Map

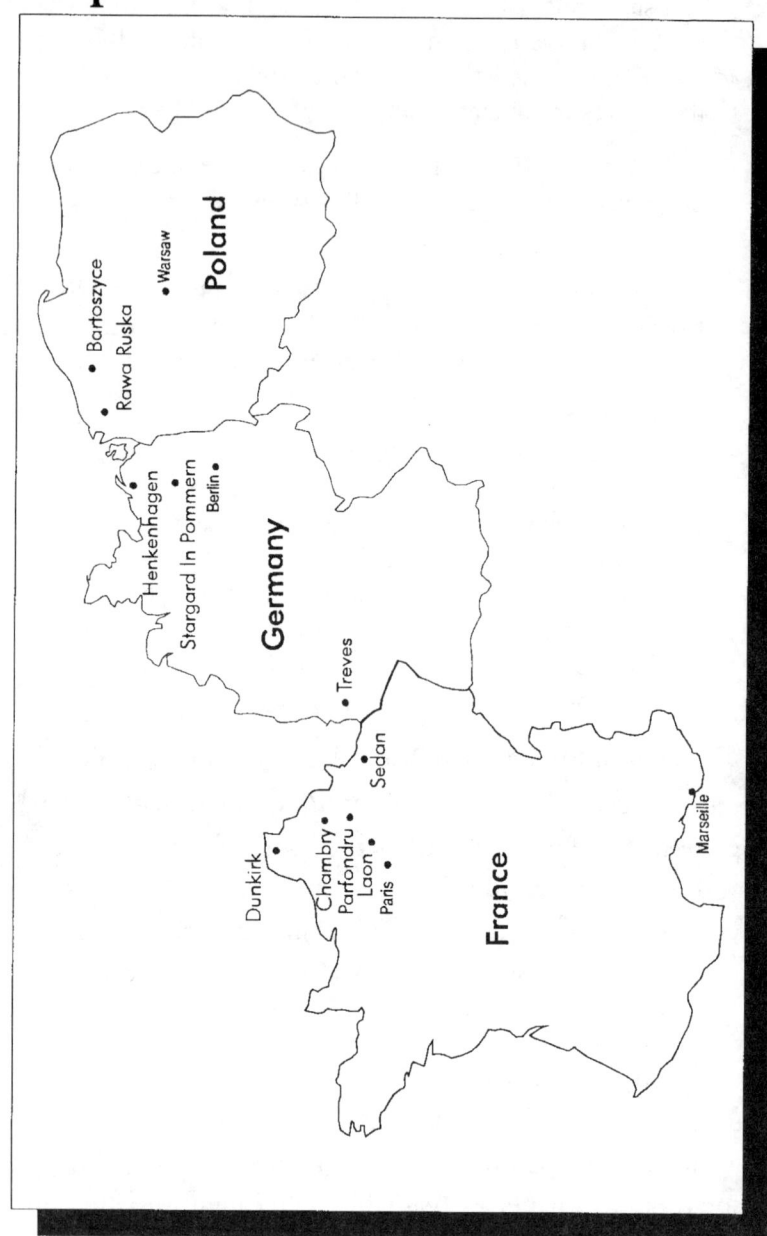

Impact Christian Books

332 Leffingwell Ave., Suite 101
Kirkwood, MO 63122

AVAILABLE AT YOUR LOCAL BOOKSTORE, OR YOU MAY ORDER DIRECTLY. Toll-Free, order-line only M/C, DISC, or VISA 1-800-451-2708.

Visit our Website at *www.impactchristianbooks.com*

Write for *FREE* Catalog.